Masonic Questions and Answers

by Paul M. Bessel

Masonic Questions and Answers

A Cornerstone Book
Copyright © 2005 by Paul M. Bessel

Published by Cornerstone Book Publishers
Charlottesville, VA & New Orleans, LA
USA.

First Cornerstone Edition - 2005

www.cornerstonepublishers.com

ISBN: 1-887560-59-9

MADE IN THE USA

Introduction

When George H. Chapin was in the Grand Line in Virginia he selected a committee to assist him to prepare a series of three booklets that would be used for candidate instruction. George felt the old method of having candidates memorize catechisms might not be the most effective way to teach new Masons what Freemasonry is all about.

He proposed a new system of candidate proficiency that includes (a) memorization of the parts of the catechism dealing with Masonic due guards, signs, words, and tokens, (b) detailed study and explanation, in the candidates' own words, of the meaning of the Masonic obligations, and (c) working with coaches in reading and discussing booklets with Masonic questions and answers appropriate for Entered Apprentices, Fellowcrafts, and Master Masons.

This last requirement was intended to be as intensive and probably as time consuming as the old catechism memorization. The purpose. The purpose was to spend this time with a coach, bonding just as much as in the old system but with the candidate and coach discussing each of the questions and answers and using them to launch into further discussions of Masonry and the Lodge into which the candidate was entering.

The three booklets with questions and answers were well received and have been used even in Lodges that decided to continue to use the old long memorization system.

When Michael Poll, the owner of Cornerstone Book Publishers, spoke with me about the need for a book that would help new Masons learn basic information about Freemasonry I thought of how the three Virginia booklets could be adapted for this purpose. The current Grand Master of Virginia, John R. Quinley, was kind enough to give his approval, and the result is the *Masonic Questions and Answers* you will find following this introduction.

Of course, every Mason could select a different list of questions and some might feel that some answers are not what they would have written, but that is a matter of individual judgment. Michael Poll, a very good friend in addition to being the editor and publisher of this work, provided extremely helpful suggestions but of course the final work and any problems or inaccuracies, perceived or real, are my sole responsibility.

I hope new Masons will use these questions and answers as a starting point. Do not read this book in private. Get together with other Masons in Lodges or elsewhere to discuss these subjects. Use this work to help launch you and other Brethren into the vast world of Masonic history, philosophy, organization, symbolism, and self-improvement. Always question and seek more information and Freemasonry will be as meaningful for you as it has been for millions of Brethren who have taken this path before us.

Paul M. Bessel
Silver Spring, Maryland
October, 2005

Thanks
to Dad, Mom, and Denise
and to the Brethren of the
Grand Lodge of the District of Columbia

Table of Contents

Masonic Questions and Answers

The
Entered Apprentice
Degree

EA-1. What is the official definition of Freemasonry?

There is no official definition, since no one person can speak officially for all of Freemasonry. Masonic writers have provided some definitions, but none is considered official by Masons everywhere. Freemasonry embraces the basic idea of allowing each man to think things through for himself and to draw conclusions which will bring him the greatest personal satisfaction. One of the most widely used and generally accepted definitions is that Freemasonry is the Brotherhood of man under the fatherhood of God. It is up to each Mason to define what Freemasonry means to him.

EA-2. What are some ideas of what Freemasonry is?

One common definition is that Freemasonry is a system of morality, veiled in allegory, and illustrated by symbols, but some do not find this very helpful. Some feel that Freemasonry is primarily intended to help each Mason improve himself to be a better person. Some refer to Freemasonry as a way of life or as an organization to make good men better. Other Masonic scholars have focused on Freemasonry as a way to learn more about God's plan for each of us. Recently, more Masonic writers have said Freemasonry is primarily a method for humanity to learn to live together in society in a peaceful manner, by emphasizing tolerance and the responsibility of each person to help others. Each Mason can use some or all of these definitions to decide what Masonry is for him. Most Masons would probably agree that Freemasonry is a fraternity that has existed for centuries, and attempts to bring in as members men who are of good character and who want to improve themselves and help society become a better place for us all.

EA-3. Why do men join Freemasonry?

For many different reasons. Many are interested in fellowship, the social setting of getting to know more good men and sharing time with them. Others want to learn more about Masonic philosophy and ideals, and how to improve themselves. Many want to perform more charitable work in their communities. Some want to do several of these things in the context of an organization that has existed for centuries attempting to do good in society.

EA-4. What are the main characteristics of Freemasonry?

It is a charitable organization in the sense that it is not organized for profit or for the financial benefit of its members or anyone else. It is devoted to the betterment of each man and of all society. It is benevolent because it teaches helping others as a duty. It is educational in that it teaches by certain ceremonies and rituals, lessons promoting morality and brotherhood. It is religious only in the sense that men who profess to believe in Deity, or a Supreme Being, are admitted as members, and because Masonry urges each man to practice his own religion. It is a social organization because it promotes brotherly interactions and fraternal enjoyment of the company of its members.

EA-5. How does Freemasonry attempt to achieve its goals?

Masonic ritual in the three degrees teaches us lessons about how people should interact with one another. Morality, charity, and tolerance toward all people are taught through the use of symbols and allegories, which are fictional stories that teach lessons. Freemasonry also teaches men to be better by showing examples of Masons who practiced and continue to practice the precepts of helping other people, accepting all as brothers, and promoting democracy and freedom for all.

EA-6. What are the goals and teachings of Freemasonry?

There is general acceptance that the goals of Freemasonry include making men into better people, being more moral and helpful in their communities. Freemasonry teaches basic values: honesty and fair dealings with everyone, charity and help for those in need, and controlling our passions. Most of all, Freemasonry teaches us to remember that we are all the children of God, brothers and sisters with all humanity, regardless of race, color, religious or political beliefs, gender, physical or financial condition, or any other outward differences.

EA-7. Aren't these teachings so basic that we don't need Freemasonry to promote them?

It sometimes seems that everyone says they support these goals, but unfortunately many do not follow them. This has been true in all times. The lessons of Freemasonry are that it may sometimes be difficult, for example, to be honest and fair in every way with every person we meet, but we must strive to meet this ideal. We might forget about people needing moral support, such as those who are ill and lonely, those needing financial help, and those needing our support to help them accomplish an important task. Even if it might sometimes be difficult for us to give this support, Freemasonry teaches that we should try to provide it.

EA-8. How did Freemasonry start, and how did it evolve?

No one knows how Freemasonry started. It is a Masonic tradition that the builders of cathedrals and other large buildings in the middle ages formed guilds, which later accepted others as members. The builders were called operative Masons, and those who use builders' tools to teach moral lessons were called speculative Masons. Speculative means those who think about such things as philosophy: why man is here, what is our purpose in life, and how we should live our lives. Traditionally, over time speculative Masons came to dominate the operative Lodges, and eventually they formed Freemasonry as we know it today.

EA-9. How did Masonry, as we know it now, start?

In 1717 in London, England, representatives of four Masonic Lodges met together and formed the first Grand Lodge. Of course, Masonic Lodges existed before then, or else how would those four Lodges have started, but no one knows any further details for sure, before 1717. Since that date, we have fairly clear records about the history of Freemasonry.

EA-10. How did Freemasonry grow since 1717?

The Grand Lodge formed in 1717 in London started new Lodges by granting them Charters, or Dispensations. Some Lodges in turn formed new Grand Lodges in more countries, until now Freemasonry exists in almost all parts of the world. There are estimated to be about 4 million Masons in the world, with about 2 million of them in the United States. There are Grand Lodges in each of the states of the U.S. and the District of Columbia, with about 13,000 chartered Lodges under them. In addition, there are other Masonic Grand Lodges and Lodges that are part of different systems or branches of Freemasonry, such as Prince Hall which consists mostly of African-American Masons, and Co-Masonry which includes both men and women members. Most Grand Lodges in our branch of Freemasonry, which is sometimes called mainstream Freemasonry, recognize Prince Hall Masonry but none recognize any form of Masonry that includes women..

EA-11. What is meant by Ancients and Moderns in Freemasonry?

After the first Grand Lodge was founded in London in 1717, some Masons came to feel that this Grand Lodge was not doing what it should. They founded another Grand Lodge in England, which called itself the Ancients or Antients, because they felt they were preserving the older traditions of Freemasonry. The other group was called the Moderns even though it was older than the Ancients. These two rival Grand Lodges existed in England for about 80 years, and each one chartered Lodges in North America and elsewhere, until they merged in 1813 and became the United Grand Lodge of England which exists to this day.

EA-12. How did Freemasonry develop in our country?

Soon after Freemasonry began its modern existence in London in 1717, Masons started coming to what were then the colonies in North America and founding Lodges here. Some of these Lodges were chartered by one of the Grand Lodges in England, and others were founded by the Grand Lodges of Scotland or Ireland. Still others were founded by Masons without a charter from any Grand Lodge. Masonry grew in America, and after the American Revolution Grand Lodges were founded in each of the States in our country, plus the

District of Columbia, with the lodges in each state and D.C. being under the jurisdiction of the Grand Lodge of that jurisdiction.

EA-13. What occurs in Masonic Lodge meetings?

At some meetings we conduct the Masonic ritual. This consists of certain specified words and plays, called degrees, that are designed to teach the moral lessons of Freemasonry. At other Lodge meetings we have speakers and discussions to promote Masonic education and the development of the Lodge members to be better people, and also conduct the business of the Lodges.

EA-14. What happens in Masonic Degrees?

The candidate (the person who will become the new member) is conducted by Lodge members during the Degree where he is the central character in the play. He is treated in the most kindly and respectful way at all times. There is no hazing or harm of any sort. During the progress of the Degree the candidate is expected to observe and listen to everything going on around him, so he can learn some of the moral and character-building lessons of Freemasonry. These lessons are so important, and there are so many deep meanings in many of the Degrees, that many Masons watch the Masonic Degrees being given to others for years and learn more each time they see them performed.

EA-15. What does it mean to say that Masons are Brothers?

> Freemasonry teaches that there is a special bond between Masons, brought about by our shared experiences with Masonic ritual and teachings. Freemasons should make an extra effort to help each other, to support each other in every way, to try to do everything we can to assist our Brother Masons. We try not to become angry with another Mason, but if we do, we should go out of our way to resolve our differences in a way that makes everyone happy. We should never harm a Brother Mason or anyone else. We should always seek to treat our Brethren exactly as we would want them to treat us.

EA-16. Does this idea of brotherhood extend further?

> Very definitely! Masons are taught that the principles of Freemasonry are to extend even further. Every Mason should treat every human being with respect, honor, kindness, charity, and friendship.

EA-17. What is meant by Enlightenment in Freemasonry?

> For Masons, enlightenment means improvement by learning in order to become better people. The Enlightenment was a period of history, during the 18th century, when society seemed to take more of an interest in concepts such as using science and logic to improve society, using rational thinking. Prior to that, society in general appeared static to many, but the Enlighten-

ment was a concept that each man, and all of society, can improve. Many feel the Enlightenment led directly to such historical events as the American and French Revolutions, and greater freedom for all individuals. Some feel that Freemasonry is a product of the Enlightenment, and in fact is the very embodiment of the concepts that became accepted at that time.

EA-18. What is meant by the universalism of Freemasonry?

Freemasonry's philosophy seeks the attainment of the objective of improving men by teaching tolerance, and acceptance of people on a universal basis, without regard to race, nationality, sect, opinion, politics, or anything other than each person's inner qualities.

EA-19. What role has Freemasonry played in the history of our country?

Many of the prominent figures of the American Revolution, such as George Washington and Benjamin Franklin, were Masons, and the ideals of Freemasonry, such as democracy and individual freedom, are similar to those upon which our country was founded. George Washington wrote many letters showing his support for Freemasonry, and Benjamin Franklin was a Grand Master of Pennsylvania. Throughout our country's history, many of those who were prominent were also Masons, including 14 of the 42 men who have been Presidents. Harry S. Truman was Grand Master of Missouri, and he was a very enthusiastic Freemason throughout his adult life.

EA-20. *What is the ritual of Freemasonry and where did it come from?*

Ritual is a word used to mean the words and ceremonies used in Masonic Lodges to open and close our meetings, confer Degrees, and do our other work in a manner considered proper for Masons. The Masonic ritual is somewhat different in each state and country. No one knows for sure where it came from, but in its present form it started in England in the early 1700s. It has changed, but not much, since then.

EA-21. *Why is the language of Masonic ritual different from ordinary language?*

Since our ritual is derived from the ritual of the 1700s and earlier, some of the language is that which was common in that earlier period. Our daily language has changed, but the Masonic ritual often maintains the older words for the sake of tradition.

EA-22. *How did our Masonic ritual develop?*

In the late 1700s, William Preston, an Englishman, rewrote and compiled much of the Masonic ritual that until then was different in each Lodge. In America, in the early 1800s, Thomas Smith Webb rewrote much of the Preston ritual for use here. Over the years, some changes have continued to be made in the Masonic ritual, so the ritual in each state is different. Still, Masons visiting Lodges in other states can recognize different rituals because of their basic similarity. In some other countries, Masonic ritual is very different from ours, and in some, such as England, different Lodges in the same jurisdiction have different rituals.

EA-23. What does the term Entered Apprentice mean?

Entered Apprentice (EA) refers to someone who has received the 1st Degree in Freemasonry. The words refer to the old days when builders had learners or beginners who were learning their work, and called them apprentices. Often these were young men, of good reputation, who were required to be obedient and willing to listen and learn. It is said that apprentices were brought into Lodges of builders to be evaluated by the members, and if they were accepted they were considered to be Entered Apprentices in the Lodge, and allowed to learn the Craft.

EA-24. Why do we use this term now?

Freemasonry uses many terms that go back to the days of operative Masons, meaning those who actually built the cathedrals and other large buildings in Europe. The Entered Apprentices of those days are symbolized by the Entered Apprentices in Masonic Lodges today, meaning those who have just begun their instruction in Freemasonry.

EA-25. What happens to Entered Apprentices?

In the past, the builders' apprentices were expected to learn the building craft, and if they did that successfully, they were advanced. Similarly in our Lodges today, if an Entered Apprentice learns what he is expected to about Freemasonry, he will advance to the other Masonic Degrees.

EA-26. What is expected of Entered Apprentices today?

EA's are expected to show obedience to the rules of Freemasonry, humility in their speech and actions, and industriousness in learning more about Freemasonry.

EA-27. Where is someone first prepared to become a Mason?

In his heart, because becoming a Mason involves a commitment to work to become a better person and to help to make the world a better place. The heart, figuratively speaking, is the seat of man's affections and desires. Freemasonry is about building better character, so the first thing anyone must do to become a Mason is to be prepared in his heart to become a better person. This may sound easy, but it often is not.

EA-28. How are EA's then prepared?

They are said to be duly and truly prepared. This means wearing special garments furnished by the Lodge to emphasize our concern with the equality of all candidates, and our interest in a man's internal qualities rather than his ability or lack of ability to have expensive clothing. Duly and truly prepared also means not having certain items on your person, and wearing clothes in a certain way.

EA-29. Why are these things done?

Most of the lessons of Freemasonry are taught by the use of symbols. Many of the ways in which men are prepared for their Degrees, and all of what goes on during the conferral of the Degrees, is meant to symbolize various things about how to be a better person and how to help others to become better people.

EA-30. What is a hoodwink?

It is a blindfold. People are often blind-folded to symbolize darkness, or the state of not having yet learned certain lessons. It is meant to symbolize the fact that before becoming a Mason a man has not yet had the opportunity to learn the lessons of Freemasonry.

EA-31. What is a cable tow?

A cable tow is a piece of rope that is placed in a certain specified way, to symbolize various things. It is a symbol of the external restraints that are placed upon all of us during our lives, and which we should try to rise above. It also means the length to which we should try to do certain things. In another sense, the cable tow symbolizes the tie that connects every Mason to every other Mason, and it is as long and as strong as each Mason determines it to be.

EA-32. What happens in the EA Degree at the entrance of a Lodge?

Certain actions are taken by or on behalf of the candidate, and certain responses are given. Specific questions are asked, and specific answers are required. This teaches that a new Mason is going through an important process, his initiation into Freemasonry.

EA-33. Is a man ever harmed in any way in a Masonic Lodge?

Never. No matter what a man says or does, even if he decides not to proceed in Freemasonry, he is never physically or mentally harmed in any way in a Masonic Lodge. There is no place in Masonic ceremonies for horseplay or hazing. The ritual of Freemasonry is serious and solemn, inculcating spiritual lessons with great dignity.

EA-34. What is the meaning of the manner in which a man is received when he enters a Lodge in the EA Degree?

When the Senior Deacon stops the candidate just after he enters the Lodge, a ceremony is performed that symbolically, never physically, shows the significance of his entrance into the Lodge. This symbolizes the importance of the obligations to which he will shortly be asked if he agrees. It also reminds each man that every act each of us takes has consequences, rewards or penalties.

EA-35. Why does Masonry ask in whom a candidate puts his trust?

A fundamental principle of Freemasonry is a belief in God. It is necessary for each candidate to say he puts his trust in God in order to become a Mason. However, no Mason is to ask any further questions about any other Mason's religious beliefs. If a man says he believes in God, we take him at his word. Masonry respects each man's religious beliefs, whether he is Christian, Jewish, Moslem, Hindu, Buddhist, or he believes in any other religious faith.

EA-36. What is meant by the Holy Saints John and the dedication of Lodges?

Freemasonry has some myths that we recognize as not being true, but which are repeated because of tradition. We say that EA's are from a Lodge of the Holy Saints John, referring to John the Baptist and John the Evangelist. These were said to be patron saints of builders in the Middle Ages, and modern Masonic Lodges keep up this tradition. We recognize, of course, that these saints were not Masons, and that they did not belong to a Lodge in Jerusalem. It is also important to note that men whose religions do not include a belief in saints are

very welcome in Freemasonry. The refer-
ences to the Saints John are symbolic of
what was said in the past.

EA-37. What do the directional indications in Lodges mean?

The East refers to the place in the Lodge
where the presiding officer, who is called
the Worshipful Master, sits. Symbolically,
this is the place from which light or learning
comes. This does not necessarily mean that
the Worshipful Master has to sit in the
eastern part of the room. Wherever he sits is
called the East of the Lodge. The Senior
Warden sits in the West, and the Junior
Warden in the South. No officer of the
Lodge sits in the North, which is considered
the dark place in the Lodge. There are
various symbolic explanations for this.

EA-38. What is the altar for in Lodges?

The altar is in the center of each Masonic
Lodge, to indicate that it is symbolically the
center of the universe, the place where
candidates are brought to light. Upon it are
placed the Holy Bible, the square, and the
compasses. If a candidate or Mason
worships upon a different holy book, that
book is placed on the altar in addition to the
Holy Bible. The spiritual and intellectual
truths of Masonry are indicated by those
items called the Great Lights: the Holy
Bible, the square, and the compasses.

EA-39. Does Freemasonry consider certain books, religions, or prayers, to be holy?

Most Grand Lodges requires that the Holy Bible be open on the altar of every Lodge. At the same time, Freemasonry teaches the quality of tolerance, meaning that we should all accept the fact that each person worships God in his own way. None of us have the right to say that another man's method of worshiping is either right or wrong. Freemasonry is a way for men to learn to live in peace with each other, even when we belong to different religions. Therefore, Freemasonry teaches that whatever book a man considers holy is the book he should use. In Masonic Lodges, all prayers are non-denominational and every man is accepted regardless of his religion.

EA-40. What are the square and compasses for?

They have many symbolic meanings in Freemasonry, and when placed together they form the most common symbol of Freemasonry. They are placed on the altar, on the Holy Bible, to symbolize lessons about man bettering himself. The square symbolizes morality, truthfulness, and honesty. The compasses symbolize self-restraint, skill, and knowledge.

EA-41. What does the Lodge represent?

The world. In another sense it represents the universality of Masonry and the extent of a Mason's charity toward the imperfections and faults of others.

EA-42. What is the Masonic obligation?

Obligation is another word for oath or promise. In the Masonic Degrees, candidates are asked if they will agree to be obligated to certain things, such as helping their fellow Masons and fellow humans. This is the heart of each Degree, and is considered very solemn and important. It is an outward sign of a man's sincerity. If a man violates any of his promises, especially a Masonic obligation, other Masons consider him to be without honor and not worthy of respect.

EA-43. What else happens if a man violates any of his Masonic obligations?

He might be reprimanded, suspended, or expelled from Freemasonry, and his former Masonic Brethren might consider him disgraced, but that is all. No man is ever to be harmed, physically or mentally, by Freemasons, even if he has violated any of his promises in Freemasonry.

EA-44. Why are some physical penalties included in Masonic obligations?

Freemasonry often follows traditions, sometimes just for the sake of tradition. Centuries ago people sometimes swore to do certain things, and said they were so serious that if they did not keep their promises they hoped they would die, or suffer certain penalties. In Masonic Lodges the obligations retain such statements, but they are purely symbolic of the seriousness of the promises being made. No Mason or former Mason is ever harmed physically, even if he violates his Masonic obligations.

EA-45. What is the Masonic apron for?

The Masonic apron has many symbolic meanings. Builders' apprentices in olden times wore aprons to protect their clothing. Some say Masons wear their aprons to symbolize the fact that we are trying to protect our characters, and improve them. Some say the apron was a symbol that the wearer owed service to another, and thus symbolizes today that Freemasons owe a duty to help their fellow men. Another symbolic meaning is that man is made up of a physical nature and a spiritual nature. The white color of the apron symbolizes innocence and purity, characteristics of a man's nature for which we should strive. Masons sometimes say the Masonic apron is more honorable than any other decoration we could receive, because of the importance of the lessons Masons are taught about character-building.

EA-46. What is the rite of destitution?

When candidates are brought into the Lodge, they are asked to remove any metals or minerals that might be on their person, in imitation of ancient practices during initiations. In modern Lodges it teaches that Masons should not bring anything into Lodges which might disturb the peace and harmony of the Lodge, and that we are all viewed as equals in the Lodge, regardless of what we might or might not own. Symbolically, this also teaches that every man should leave his passions and prejudices outside the Lodge, and he should work to eliminate prejudices and to restrain passions. Also, the rite of destitution teaches that even when a man does not have minerals or metals, meaning items that are considered precious, he should still try to help his fellow men who might be poorer than he is. Charity is one of the most important lessons of Freemasonry.

EA-47. Why are EA's placed in the northeast corner of Lodges?

Traditionally, the northeast corner is the foundation of a building, the place where construction begins, where the cornerstone is laid. An Entered Apprentice is considered to be starting his process of building his Temple, or character, so he is placed in the northeast corner at the start of his Masonic journey. It also symbolizes that he is midway between the symbolic darkness of the North and the light of the east. He has left the darkness of the rest of the world and is moving toward more light, or knowledge, symbolized by the East.

EA-48. What are the working tools of Entered Apprentices, and why?

The working tools are the 24-inch gauge and common gavel. These tools were used by operative builders to construct their works, but in Freemasonry they are said to have more noble, symbolic meanings. The 24-inch gauge is to teach us to use the hours of the day for important purposes, improving our lives and the lives of those around us. The common gavel is said to be used symbolically to smooth out the rough spots in our characters, so we can become better people, living stones that will be able to build a better Temple or character.

EA-49. Why is there a lecture at the end of the Degree?

There are lessons in the Degree which might not be obvious, and there also is additional information which Masons think is useful to tell candidates. This information is imparted in lectures after the Degrees.

EA-50. What can an Entered Apprentice do in Masonry?

EA's can attend EA Lodge meetings, and are entitled to some other rights of Masons but usually cannot vote or hold office until they complete the remaining two degrees. EA's do have the right, indeed the duty, to learn more about Freemasonry and to become proficient in the EA Degree. When an EA has learned what is required of him he is then given the Fellowcraft, or second,

Degree in Masonry, followed by the Master Mason, or third, Degree.

EA-51. What are Lodges and Grand Lodges?

Masons gather in groups that are called Lodges. Each Lodge usually consists of several dozen or even hundreds of Masons who enjoy each other's company and who meet regularly, usually once a month but sometimes more or less often, to conduct their business, plan their activities, and conduct programs such as listening to speakers on topics such as Masonic philosophy or history, and conduct Degree work. Lodge meetings must include a certain number of Master Masons assembled in the Lodge room, with a Holy Bible, Square, and Compasses on the altar, and with a Charter or Dispensation in the room. Grand Lodges are the groups that establish Lodges by granting them Charters or Dispensations, and make the rules governing Freemasonry in each jurisdiction.

EA-52. What does tiling mean?

That is another word for closing the Lodge door and keeping the meeting private to all except Masons. The Lodge officer who stands just outside the door, to permit Masons to enter but keep non-Masons out, is called the Tiler. This is sometimes spelled Tyler.

EA-53. Who are the main Lodge officers?

The Worshipful Master (*worshipful* means honorable) is the leader of the Lodge. The next officers are the Senior Warden and the Junior Warden. These three are called the Stationed Officers.

EA-54. Who are the other Lodge officers?

The Treasurer and Secretary have duties in a Lodge that are obvious from their titles. The Senior Deacon and Junior Deacon have specific responsibilities, including carrying messages among the Stationed Officers, conducting candidates during Degrees, greeting visiting Masons, and closing (or tiling) the door.

EA-55. Are there additional Lodge officers?

Some Lodges have a Marshal, who conducts public ceremonies, an Organist or Musician, who plays music during Lodge meetings and Degrees, and additional officers to help conduct the business of the Lodge.

EA-56. What is meant by line officers?

In most Lodges, officers progress from each position to the next higher position in the Lodge each year. For example, the Junior Deacon usually becomes Senior Deacon the following year, then Junior Warden, Senior Warden, and finally Worshipful Master. That is why the group of officers is sometimes referred to as the progressive line.

EA-57. How are Lodge officers selected?

Each Grand Lodge has its own rules about how Lodges elect or appoint officers. In most jurisdictions, the Worshipful Master, Senior Warden, Junior Warden, Secretary, and Treasurer, are elected by the Brethren. Some Grand Lodge codes also specify that the Senior and Junior Deacon are elected, some state that other officers, such as Stewards and the Tiler, are also elected, and some Grand Lodges allow each Lodge to decide for itself which officers are elected and which are appointed by the Worshipful Master.

EA-58. What is the role of the Worshipful Master of the Lodge?

He is similar to the president of an organization, but with greater powers. That is why he is often referred to as Worshipful, which means Honorable. Even though a Worshipful Master has great powers in his Lodge, he must constantly think about and promote the good of the Lodge as a whole and all its members, and must operate pursuant to the rules of the Grand Lodge under which his Lodge operates. The Worshipful Master is responsible for arranging the programs in the Lodge, seeing that the Degrees are conferred properly, and in every other way insuring the successful operation of the Lodge.

EA-59. Why does the Worshipful Master wear a hat in the Lodge?

Since the Worshipful Master is in charge of the Lodge, he wears a hat to symbolize his authority. Sometimes it is said that the Worshipful Master wears a hat to symbolize his rank, or in imitation of the crown worn by King Solomon.

EA-60. How do you know when to rise and when to be seated in a Lodge?

In general, when the Worshipful Master raps his gavel once, that is to indicate that all the Brethren should be seated, quiet, and in order. When the Worshipful Master raps twice, that means the officers of the Lodge, and only the officers, should stand. When the Worshipful Master raps three times, that means that everyone in the Lodge should stand. When all are standing and the Worshipful Master raps once, that means that everyone should be seated. Also, if the Worshipful Master addresses a member of the Lodge by name, or if he, for example, calls on all Entered Apprentices, that means they should stand, salute the Worshipful Master and listen to instructions. If you wish to speak in Lodge, or if you need to leave the Lodge before it is closed, you should wait for an appropriate time, then rise, wait until the Worshipful Master recognizes you, and then salute the Worshipful Master and speak.

EA-61. Can a Mason enter a Lodge meeting after it has begun?

Yes. To do this you identify yourself to the Tiler outside the door and then wait until the Tiler can inform the Lodge that you want to enter. When you enter the Lodge, you should walk to the altar, salute the Worshipful Master, and then follow his instructions.

EA-62. What is the role of prayer in Lodges, and how are prayers offered?

Masonic Lodges have prayer at the beginning and end of their meetings, and sometimes during meetings such as when we are remembering a member who has recently died. Prayers are usually offered by the Chaplain or the Worshipful Master, and are always to be non-sectarian. Masons offer their prayers to the Great Architect of the Universe, meaning the God that each of us individually recognizes. At the end of prayers Masons say, So mote it be, which means So may it ever be, indicating that we agree with the intent of the prayer.

EA-63. Why do we use signs, tokens, and passwords?

Freemasonry, just as other organizations, has ways of identifying its members to one another. It is important for Freemasons to memorize the signs, tokens, and passwords, so we can prove to other Masons that we are Masons. Also, each of the signs, tokens, and passwords has a symbolic meaning and teaches us something important about Masonic philosophy. Understanding how to do the signs, tokens, and passwords properly, and executing them with dignity, is an important way to show respect for Freemasonry. Masons should understand that we have given our word not to disclose the signs, tokens, and passwords of Freemasonry to non-Masons, but for over 200 years books have been published in which these secrets are disclosed, often with pictures.

EA-64. What are Masons supposed to keep secret, and what can we tell others about Freemasonry?

Almost everything about Freemasonry can, and should, be discussed by Masons with their family, friends, and others. We should proudly tell everyone about the ideals of Freemasonry, its history, its support of brotherhood and charity, its promotion of democracy, individual rights, and opposition to bigotry and prejudice in any form. Masons can also tell others about when and where meetings are held, who are the members and officers, and just about anything else — except to tell or show non-Masons the signs, tokens, and passwords, or the exact complete wording of the rituals. Therefore, there are very few secrets in Freemasonry, and it is not really a secret organization in any way.

EA-65. Does a Mason have an obligation to attend Lodge meetings?

Masons should attend as many Lodge meetings as they can. However, there is no attendance requirement, and no penalty for failing to attend a certain number of meetings.

EA-66. *Are there subjects that cannot be discussed in Lodges?*

Yes. Religion and politics are prohibited subjects in Lodges, and, as a matter of good taste, around Lodge meetings. These two subjects can cause disputes and disharmony. One of the main points of Freemasonry is to provide an oasis from the discord and divisiveness of the world, where men can come together and enjoy each other's company in peace and harmony.

EA-67. *Where can you find the rules that govern activities in each Lodge?*

Grand Lodges have books of rules that are usually called the Code of that jurisdiction. These rules govern how the Grand Lodge operates, how each Lodge operates, and how individual Masons are expected to act. Each Lodge also has bylaws, which describe certain procedures that must be followed by that Lodge. Also, there are Masonic traditions that each Mason and group of Masons is expected to follow. These are learned by experience rather than reading them in a book.

EA-68. *What are actions that are considered un-Masonic?*

Criminal actions, particularly those involving violations of fundamental moral laws, are un-Masonic. Violations of the obligations in the Degrees would be considered un-Masonic, as would violations of any of the requirements of each jurisdiction's Code and of the high moral standards that are expected of Freemasons.

EA-69. What are the key questions every Entered Apprentice should be able to answer?

What is Freemasonry?

What are some of the goals and teachings of Freemasonry?

What is a Masonic Lodge?

Who are the key officers in each Lodge?

Who is the presiding officer in a Lodge, and what are his responsibilities and authority?

What is the difference between operative and speculative masons?

Is Masonry a secret organization?

What are the few secrets, and what are the many subjects Masons are encouraged to talk about?

Are men of every religion permitted to become Masons?

What is the one religious requirement in Freemasonry?

How does a man prepare himself to become a Mason?

What is the purpose of the altar and the items contained on it in Lodges?

What is the EA obligation for, and what should we learn from it?

What is an Entered Apprentice supposed to do in Freemasonry?

What does an EA need to know about basic protocol in Lodges?

EA-70. What are some books Entered Apprentices can read to learn more about Freemasonry?

> *The Craft and Its Symbols*
> by Allen E. Roberts, published in 1974
>
> *Introduction to Freemasonry*
> by Carl H. Claudy, published in 1931
>
> *A Comprehensive View of Freemasonry*
> by Henry W. Coil, published in 1954
>
> *Masonic Philanthropies: A Tradition of Caring,*
> by S. Brent Morris
> 2nd edition published in 1997
>
> *Masonic Membership of the Founding Fathers*
> by Ronald E. Heaton, published in 1965
>
> *Freemasonry in American History*
> by Allen E. Roberts, published in 1985

The
Fellowcraft
Degree

FC-1. What is the essence of Freemasonry?

It is the intellectual tradition of Freemasonry, especially the Fellowcraft Degree, which teaches us to improve our minds, to learn more. Masonic scholar and author William Moseley Brown said, "Whenever you become a champion of the mind's right to be free; whenever you are an enemy of bigotry or intolerance ... you live the teachings of the Degree of Fellowcraft."

FC-2. Why is education important in Freemasonry?

Education is necessary to progress. Each individual's life is limited, so if all we knew was what we learned in our personal contacts we would be poorly equipped to deal with the complexities and responsibilities of life. Through education we can add the experience of others to our own, and come to possess a greater knowledge of man and life.

FC-3. What is the purpose of symbolism in Freemasonry?

It is to stimulate each Mason to search for light, for education, for himself. The symbols and emblems reveal the truth, but only when each of us seeks and finds it for himself. Only when a man finds truth for himself does it remain his permanent possession.

FC-4. What are allegories?

> Fictional stories that are supposed to teach us lessons if we think about them.

FC-5. What is the most important lesson of the Fellowcraft Degree?

> Each person is a unique individual entitled to dignity and respect, and each of us should do his best to learn, to improve our mind, to improve our character, and to help humanity, which is a brotherhood of all men under the fatherhood of the Supreme Being.

FC-6. What are the principles of individual freedom that Freemasonry supports?

> Freemasonry teaches that each individual is a child of God, and an equal to every other individual. Although each of us may have a different religion, we are entitled to be respected for our individual beliefs. Similarly, we may have disagreements about political issues, but Freemasonry teaches that we should be tolerant of each other's views. In Masonic Lodges no discussion of religion or politics is permitted, as this could lead to discord in a setting where we strive for harmony and brotherhood.

FC-7. What is the role of freedom in Freemasonry?

> A fundamental concept of Freemasonry since its beginning has been the freedom of

each individual to act on his own, to develop as he sees fit, free of undue restraints. Freemasonry opposes totalitarianism in any form, and promotes democracy and freedom. It teaches support for freedom of speech, freedom of conscience, and freedom of thought.

FC-8. What does the FC Degree symbolize?

The Fellowcraft Degree is meant to symbolize man in his prime years, in the sense that the EA Degree symbolizes youth.

FC-9. What are the themes of the FC Degree?

Education and achievement are the themes. The more a man learns through the pursuit of knowledge, the more he achieves and the better he becomes.

FC-10. What instrument is used to receive a candidate for the FC Degree, and what is its significance?

The square is the instrument that first touches the FC candidate, and we are taught to use it to be the rule and guide of all our actions toward mankind. This means we should be moral, fair, and honest toward all people.

FC-11. How is the FC obligation different from the EA obligation?

The basic point of the EA obligation was fidelity to Freemasonry. In the FC obligation we are asked to swear that we will act in proper ways with our Brethren in Freemasonry. The penalties described in the FC Degree are just as symbolic as those in the EA Degree. The only thing that can happen to a man who violates any of his Masonic oaths is that he can be reprimanded, suspended, or expelled from Freemasonry, and viewed as lacking in good character. No man is ever harmed physically or mentally in Freemasonry.

FC-12. What are the working tools of the FC Degree, and what do they symbolize?

The working tools of the FC Degree are the square, plumb, and level. These instruments are used by operative Masons to make sure their work is done properly. Philosophically, these tools symbolize other things. The square is a symbol of morality, truthfulness, and honesty. When we talk in Masonry of being on the square, it means we are being honest and upright with each other. The plumb is a symbol of uprightness of conduct, just as the Holy Bible says God placed a plumbline in the midst of his people to show that they will be individually judged by standards of what is right and wrong. Masons are taught to look to the plumb as a symbol of a life lived according to a good conscience. The level is a symbol that all men are equal, and that each is to be judged by how he acts toward others, not by his wealth or looks. Every individual is endowed with a spiritual worth and dignity. Even those who hold positions of authority over others should always remember that basically we are all the same, and everyone should act toward others as he wants others to act toward him.

FC-13. What are the wages of the Fellowcraft?

Corn, wine, and oil are said to be the wages. Corn symbolizes nourishment and the sustenance of life. It is also a symbol of plenty and refers to the opportunity for doing good work for the community in which we live. Wine is symbolic of refreshment, health, spirituality, and peace. Oil represents joy, gladness, and happiness. Taken together, these three items represent the reward of living a good life.

FC-14. What are the two pillars, and what do they represent?

There were two pillars at the front of King Solomon's Temple in Biblical times, and they are said to be on the sides of the entrance to our Masonic Lodges. The pillars in King Solomon's Temple were called Boaz and Jachin, and they symbolized strength and establishment, power and control. Man must have both in his life if he is to be successful.

FC-15. What are the globes on the tops of these pillars?

They are the terrestrial globe of the Earth and the celestial globe of the stars, and are symbols of universality.

FC-16. *What is the meaning of the winding stairs?*

> They represent the progress of an inquiring mind, toiling and laboring toward intellectual progress and study. They show that we have to work hard to progress, and we need courage and faith to do so. The stairs are winding because life is an unknown. For some there will be a middle chamber filled with the reward of fame and fortune. For others it will be filled with frustration, pain, and discouragement. We climb because we have faith that the winding stairs of life lead to our destiny. We also learn that although we should constantly seek improvement and truth, we can never achieve perfection in this life.

FC-17. *What are we taught about the symbolism of the elements of the winding stairs?*

> In the Fellow Craft (or Fellowcraft) Degree we are taught that along the winding path we should study various subjects, including learning to use all our senses, and studying each of the liberal arts and sciences which impart human knowledge. We also are taught that, from the perspective of Masonic symbolism, the basic subject upon which all others are based is geometry, because everything else is built using it.

FC-18. *What does admission to the Middle Chamber represent?*

> The passage from the outer porch to the middle chamber of King Solomon's

Temple represents, symbolically, the passage from ignorance to enlightenment. The candidate in the FC Degree needs a pass, which his Brethren provide him, to enter the doors to knowledge. Man must acquire knowledge chiefly through his own efforts, but his Brethren can provide him with some help.

FC-19. What is the significance of the letter G?

G stands for geometry and also for God. This reminds us that geometry is so important in all earthly endeavors, and also that every act of ours is done in the sight of God and that Divine Providence is over all of our lives. Masons should be aware that while the most common symbol of Freemasonry in the United States is the square and compasses with the letter G in the center, the G is usually not included in the Masonic symbols in other countries.

FC-20. How are the modes of recognition of the Fellowcraft Degree different from those of the Entered Apprentice Degree?

Fellowcrafts have a different token, or handshake, a different password, and a different due guard and sign than EA's. Each of these is taught to Fellowcrafts during their Degrees, and it is important to remember them as you will be asked to show them to prove you are a Fellowcraft when you seek to enter a Fellowcraft Lodge or to salute the Worshipful Master in a Fellowcraft Lodge.

FC-21. What role did the Temple of Solomon actually play in history?

King Solomon reigned over the people of Israel about 1,000 B.C., and he built what was considered a magnificent Temple in Jerusalem to be the center of worship for his people. This Temple was destroyed by the Babylonians around 586 B.C., but when the Hebrew people returned to their land they rebuilt the Temple. Around 70 A.D., the Temple was destroyed again, and it no longer exists.

FC-22. What is the symbolism of Solomon's Temple?

Since the real Temple was the center of religion for Solomon's people, the symbolic Temple in Freemasonry is said to be the center of the divine attributes in each of us, the inner character of each of us. The Temple of Solomon was thought to be the most perfect of buildings, so our spiritual Temple can be seen as the perfection in our character that we attempt to attain. Freemasonry can be seen as indicating that each man is a living Temple where God resides, and we should do all we can to make this a more perfect Temple, physically, mentally, and spiritually. Of course, in Freemasonry each man's religious beliefs are purely his own, so each Mason can choose to interpret this symbolism as he sees fit. Freemasonry often refers to the Temple of Solomon as a symbol of what Freemasonry is all about. Symbolically, the building of the Temple means the building of better characters within each of us, and the building of a better humanity.

FC-23. What is the symbolism of the level?

Equality. Not that all men are exactly the same, but there should be equality of opportunity and rights, and we should extend goodwill, charity, tolerance, and truthfulness equally to all.

FC-24. What is needed for brotherhood?

A spiritual basis is needed, so we ask that all Masons believe in God in any way they choose. Brotherhood also requires that men be held together by unbreakable ties, hence the need for morality. Differences of beliefs and opinions must not rupture our bonds, so we must have tolerance. Men cannot be brought together easily unless they have the same rights and privileges, so we need equality. They cannot work together unless all understand the work to be done, so we need enlightenment.

FC-25. Are there books and magazines that give more information about Freemasonry?

There are thousands. Many books have been written about Masonic philosophy, history, ritual, jurisprudence, and all other aspects of Freemasonry. Many are written in a lively, popular manner, and some are very scholarly. There are also many magazines about Masonry. Many are inexpensive and informative.

FC-26. What are some good Masonic books?

Coil's Masonic Encyclopedia is one of the best places to learn about many things related to Freemasonry. A new edition was published in 1996, edited by Allen E. Roberts, who has written more Masonic books than anyone else. There are thousands of good Masonic books, many of which are listed in this book. You can find many of these Masonic books in Masonic libraries and in bookstores. Some good Masonic books were written by non-Masons. Professor Margaret C. Jacob wrote *Living the Enlightenment: Freemasonry and Politics in Eighteenth-Century Europe* and *The Radical Enlightenment: Pantheists, Freemasons and Republicans*, explaining how Freemasonry helped bring about democracy and freedom of speech. Professor Steven Bullock wrote *Revolutionary Brotherhood: Freemasonry and the Transformation of the American Social Order, 1730-1840*, which explains the role of Masonry in the early history of the United States.

FC-27. Who was Allen E. Roberts and why should Masons be proud of him?

He was the author of more Masonic books than any other Masonic author. He wrote books in language that can be understood by all, about Masonic symbolism, the meaning of the Degrees, what Freemasonry is about, Masonry in American history, and, most of all, about developing Masonic leaders. Allen E. Roberts passed away in

March 1997. His books included *The Craft and Its Symbols*, *The Mystic Tie*, *Freemasonry in American History*, *House Undivided: Freemasonry in the Civil War*, *Brother Truman*, and *G. Washington: Master Mason*.

FC-28. Who was John J. Robinson and why is he important to Freemasonry?

He was a non-Mason who wrote a book called *Born in Blood: The Lost Secrets of Freemasonry*, which described his views of how Freemasonry may have been formed by the remnants of the Knights Templar. They were a group of warrior-monks destroyed in the 1300's by the King of France and the Pope. This book had a great impact on Freemasonry, and made John J. Robinson famous. He became a frequent guest on television and radio programs, talking about the good that Masons are doing. He wrote other books about the Knights Templar and Freemasonry, and shortly before he died he became a Mason and was awarded the 33rd Degree by the Scottish Rite.

FC-29. What are some good Masonic magazines?

The Philalethes magazine, is published by the Philalethes Society, a masonic research organization, six times a year. Other magazines about Freemasonry include *The Scottish Rite Journal*, *The Royal Arch Mason*, *The Cryptic Mason*, *Knight Templar*, *The Northern Light*, and others which are mainly intended for members of each of the

Masonic appendant bodies but which contain many articles of interest to all Masons. Also, there are more detailed, excellent Masonic research journals, such as *Heredom*, the annual journal of the Scottish Rite Research Society, *Ars Quatuor Coronatorum*, usually called *AQC*, which is published by the premier Masonic research Lodge, in London, the *Transactions of the American Lodge of Research*, and of other research Lodges.

FC-30. Where can you find Masonic books and magazines?

There are several good Masonic libraries in the U.S., including those maintained at many Grand Lodge headquarters. Some of the best are at the Grand Lodge of Iowa in Cedar Rapids, the Grand Lodge of Massachusetts in Boston, the Grand Lodge of Pennsylvania in Philadelphia, the Grand Lodge of New York, and at the Scottish Rite headquarters for the Southern Jurisdiction in Washington DC and for the Northern Masonic Jurisdiction in Lexington, Massachusetts. Most Masonic libraries are open to Masons and all others interested interested in Freemasonry, and all are welcome there. You can also buy Masonic books. See Appendix E for a list of Masonic book publishers and sellers. Also, many bookstores have some Masonic books for sale, although they may be located in unusual places in these bookstores.

FC-31. How can computers be used for Masonic education?

Several computer message groups and other services provide thousands of files about Masonic subjects, Masonic pictures, and the opportunity to exchange messages with other Masons around the world. Grand Lodges encourage all Masons to learn more about Masonry, using computers as well as books and other forms of learning. The Grand Lodge has its own Internet web site, and there are hundreds of other excellent sources of Masonic education on the Internet. Masons can learn a great deal about Masonry using computers as well as books and other forms of learning. Most Grand Lodges have their own webpages and there are hundreds of other excellent sources of Masonic education on the internet. There are also many email message groups by and for Freemasons, such as those listed in Appendix C of this book. Remember that while there are good sources of Masonic information on the Internet, as well as in books and magazines, there are also sources of incorrect or completely bad information, too.

FC-32. What is the Masonic Service Association?

It is an organization based in Silver Spring, Maryland, founded and supported by almost all the Grand Lodges, that acts on behalf of all Masons to give out information, and to try to help Masons in distress because of floods, wars, or other large-scale problems. MSA also coordinates Veterans' Administration hospital visitations.

FC-33. What is the George Washington Masonic National Memorial?

This is a large building, museum, and collection of Lodge rooms, located in Alexandria, Virginia. It was built through the support of all the Grand Lodges in the United States, to honor our first President and most honored Mason, George Washington.

FC-34. How is Freemasonry involved in charity?

It may sound almost unbelievable, but Freemasons in the United States contribute about $2,000,000 every single day to charities all around the country. Masonic Lodges and other Masonic groups are involved in helping those in need of blood, those suffering from severe burns, muscular dystrophy, eye problems, severe dental diseases, and many other maladies.

FC-35. What are some examples of Masonic charity work?

The Shrine, which is made up entirely of Masons, maintains a series of hospitals for children. These Shrine hospitals provide care at no charge; they do not even have billing departments, because they never send bills to anyone. The entire cost of these hospitals, and all the doctors in them, is paid for by Masons. In fact, thousands of Masons spend untold hours driving children who need care to and from these Shrine hospitals. And this is just one example of Masonic charity work. The Scottish Rite, Southern Jurisdiction and Northern Masonic Jurisdiction, as well as Royal Arch Masonry, Cryptic Masonry, Knights Templar, Tall Cedars of Lebanon, and the Grotto, plus other Masonic groups, are all involved in many different types of charity work, as that promotes the ideals of brotherhood and community assistance.

FC-36. What are the key questions a Fellowcraft should be able to answer?

What is Freemasonry emphasizing in the FC Degree?

What should we learn from this Degree?

What does this Degree represent?

What do the square, plumb, and level symbolize?

What are the wages of the FC and what do they represent?

What are the pillars and what do they represent?

What is the meaning of the winding stairs in the FC Degree?

What is the symbolism of the Middle Chamber?

What is the letter G said to signify?

FC-37. What are some books Fellowcrafts can read to learn more about Freemasonry?

The Mystic Tie, by Allen E. Roberts, published in 1991

The Builders: A Story and Study of Freemasonry, by Joseph F. Newton, published in 1914

Cornerstones of Freedom: A Masonic Tradition, by S. Brent Morris, published in 1993

Brother Truman: The Masonic Life and Philosophy of Harry S. Truman, by Allen E. Roberts, published in 1985

Masonic Trivia and Facts, by Allen E. Roberts, published in 1994

The Great Teachings of Masonry, by H.L. Haywood, published in 1923

The Meaning of Masonry, by W.L. Wilmshurst, published in 1927

What Masonry Means, by William E. Hammond, published in 1939

Freemasons' Guide and Compendium, by Bernard E. Jones, published in 1956

Freemasonry: Its Aims & Ideals, by J.S.M. Ward, published in 1923

The
Master Mason
Degree

MM-1. *What is meant by being raised to the Sublime Degree of Master Mason?*

As a Master Mason, you are entitled to the rights and benefits of Masonry. As Master Masons, we are expected to live up to our obligations of charity and brotherhood, to support freedom of speech, thought, and conscience, and to work to eliminate any prejudices and undue passions in us. Some feel it means the raising of our consciousness to a new way of looking at how we should live our lives, with more attention to brotherhood.

MM-2. *Are there higher Degrees than Master Mason?*

Even if some Masons take Scottish Rite or York Rite Degrees, it is important to remember that the Master Mason Degree is the most important one. In a deep sense, no man ever obtains any Masonic Degree that is more important than this one.

MM-3. *What is the legend of Hiram Abif?*

This is a legend that was introduced into Masonic ceremonies after modern Freemasonry began, and that has become a central part of Masonic ritual. It is an allegory, meaning a fictional story that never really took place but which teaches us lessons about morality.

MM-4. *What lessons are taught by the legend of Hiram Abif?*

It teaches the importance of fidelity to our promises. Also, some of our worst enemies may appear to be our friends. It also teaches that we may be harmed by our own working tools, meaning our own inner qualities. Most importantly, it teaches that even if we might be harmed, there is always the hope and expectation that we may be raised up again, especially with the assistance of our Masonic Brethren.

MM-5. Why is the Master Mason Degree called sublime?

Partly because of the solemn nature of the ceremony, but also because of the profound wisdom of the lessons taught in this Degree, including the immortality of the soul.

MM-6. How is the MM Degree different from preceding Masonic Degrees?

In other degrees, the Lodge is a symbol of the world. In the MM Degree the Lodge is a representation of the Sanctum Sanctorum, or Holy of Holies, of King Solomon's Temple in Jerusalem, which itself was a symbol of heaven, a place where God dwelled. One interpretation of the MM Degree is that it teaches that to receive divine truth you must be faithful to your trust. Ultimately, you must at last die, but your soul is immortal.

MM-7. What are the symbols of the MM Degree, as compared to the other Degrees?

In the EA and FC Degrees, architecture was the theme of the symbols. The symbols of the MM Degree refer to life, its tragedies and its ultimate triumph if we lead virtuous lives. This Degree's symbols are far more spiritual.

MM-8. What is symbolized by the preparation for this degree?

The clothing reminds the candidate to be humble, to recognize that he is the same as all other candidates regardless of wealth or poverty. The candidate is also taught that as he progresses in Freemasonry his obligations become more extensive and binding. He is reminded that each man can attain his most important objectives only with the assistance of Deity and with the help given by friends and Brethren.

MM-9. What is the meaning of the reception in the Lodge room at the start of the MM Degree?

This is a reminder that all the lessons of Freemasonry must be implanted in your heart if they are to serve a useful purpose and become a part of your way of life.

MM-10. What are the working tools in the MM Degree?

They are all the implements of Masonry, more especially the trowel. The trowel is used by operative Masons to spread the cement that holds blocks together. In Masonry, we are taught the symbolic significance of the trowel. It is said to spread the cement of brotherly love that holds people together in a symbolic temple of all humanity.

MM-11. Why does Freemasonry refer to traveling in foreign countries and why are Masons sometimes referred to as traveling men?

Some say the highest goal of the operative masons of earlier centuries was to become so proficient at the knowledge and secrets of their Craft that they became master builders who could travel freely from country to country to help build great buildings wherever they lived. In speculative Freemasonry, foreign countries might refer to the fact that philosophically, all of Masonry is foreign to each new candidate. If we are to travel we must learn a new language, understand new customs and traditions, and stretch our minds to try to interpret symbols that can teach us important moral lessons.

MM-12. What is meant by traveling and earning Master's wages?

Traveling and earning Master's wages refers to studying the history and philosophy of Freemasonry to become a better person. Also, once you are a Master Mason you are permitted to travel and visit Masonic Lodges all around the world, as long as you have the proper identification and remember the methods of proving that you are a Master Mason.

MM-13. What is symbolized by the three ruffians?

There are many symbolic allusions. Anyone who attempts to obtain secrets to which they are not entitled, is guilty of a great crime. Rewards must be earned. Violence is never an acceptable form of conduct, except in self-defense. The ruffians also symbolize the passions in each of us, that we must try to keep in check. There is another symbolic explanation of the ruffians. Those who seek to enslave mankind first deny the right of free speech, which can be symbolized by a blow to the throat. The second way to try to control people is to attack their right to place their affection where they wish, and this can be symbolized by a blow to the heart. Finally, and most importantly, tyrants attack our ability to think for ourselves, and this can be symbolized by a blow to the brain.

MM-14. What is the significance of the five points of fellowship?

Brotherly love is one of the most important aspects of Freemasonry. We are taught that one of the greatest things each of us can do is help our fellow men, especially our fellow Masons, and that each of us can expect similar help from our Brethren. The five points of fellowship teach us that we should be ready, willing, and able to help our Brethren in many ways, and that we can expect similar help from them.

MM-15. What is meant by the lion of the tribe of Judah?

The lion is a symbol of might and royalty, and it was the sign of the tribe of Judah because this was the royal tribe. This was one of the titles of King Solomon. Some, because of their religious beliefs, feel this term refers to Jesus of Nazareth. Others, of different religious beliefs, feel this term refers to a coming Messiah. Each Mason can interpret this, and other symbols, as he chooses.

MM-16. *What is the lost word in Freemasonry?*

There are many interpretations, but none of us should literally look for a single word that was lost. Many feel this refers to Divine Truth, which is lost but which we are all seeking in our own way. Some feel that this means the constant search for what God intends each person to do with his life to make it worthwhile. It also means that each of us needs to triumph over any prejudices, passions, or conflicts of interest that may have developed within us. No one can be a true Freemason unless he sees each and every person, regardless of their color, race, religion, nationality, or gender, as worthy of respect and dignity. The search for the lost word also shows that Masons must always be open to receiving truth from any source, and to reexamine their opinions when they find new information. Thus, Freemasonry is devoted to freedom of thought, speech, and conscience. The idea that Masons have a substitute, and not the true lost word, indicates that we may approach the approximation of truth but never attain perfection.

MM-17. *What is the symbolism of the sprig of acacia?*

In olden days a sprig of acacia was placed

by the head of a grave to mark its location and to show a belief in the immortality of the soul. Being an evergreen, it symbolizes continuity.

MM-18. What is the symbolism of the all-seeing eye?

This is a symbol of Deity. God watches over humanity, and every man should realize that each of his acts is being weighed by the Divine against His standards of morality and virtue.

MM-19. What are appendant bodies?

Once you become a Master Mason you are eligible to join other Masonic groups, such as the Scottish Rite, Royal Arch Chapters, and others. These groups are often called appendant bodies, because membership in them is only open to those who are members in good standing in a Masonic Lodge.

MM-20. What is the Scottish Rite?

The Scottish Rite is a Masonic organization that confers Masonic degrees to teach Brethren moral lessons, just as Craft Lodges and other Masonic groups confer similar degrees. Most Masons in the U.S. receive the 4th through the 32nd Degrees in Scottish Rite conferrals, but there are some U.S. jurisdictions that confer the Scottish Rite EA, FC, and MM degrees, too. There is a Supreme Council that rules the Scottish Rite for the Southern Jurisdiction of the

United States and another for the Northern Masonic Jurisdiction. There are also two Prince Hall Supreme Councils in the U.S., and one or more Scottish Rite Supreme Councils in most countries around the world. In most places, those who are taking the Scottish Rite Degrees watch short plays, which constitute each of the Degrees and which are designed to teach more Masonic lessons. If you become a member of the Scottish Rite in the U.S., you receive the degree up to the 32nd, but the 33rd is only given to certain Masons who are selected because they have provided services, usually over a long period, to the Scottish Rite, to Freemasonry in general, or to society at large. It is a great honor to receive this Degree, no one is permitted to ask to receive it, and only about 1% of all the Scottish Rite Masons in the U.S. have received it.

MM-21. What happens in Scottish Rite Masonry?

First, there are two Scottish Rite organizations in the U.S. The Scottish Rite Supreme Council for the Southern Jurisdiction includes the states south of the Ohio River and west of the Mississippi River, and in the other states the governing body is the Scottish Rite Supreme Council for the Northern Masonic Jurisdiction. Each Scottish Rite Supreme Council is led by a Sovereign Grand Commander. State leaders are appointed, and are called Sovereign Grand Inspectors General or Deputies. Scottish Rite groups in each state are called

Orients, and in each part of a state the local group is called a Valley. The Valleys generally hold meetings monthly. Their meetings are similar to Lodge meetings, except that the rituals for opening and closing are different.

MM-22. What is the York Rite?

It is a term used to describe several different Masonic organizations that are grouped together: Royal Arch Chapters, which are sometimes called Capitular Masonry, the Cryptic Rite, and the Commandery, or Knights Templar. Also, Craft Lodges, the ones that confer the EA, FC, and MM Degrees, are considered to belong to the York Rite.

MM-23. What Degrees are in the York Rite, and how does it operate?

In most jurisdictions, Royal Arch Chapters confer 4 Degrees — Mark Master, Past Master, Most Excellent Master, and Royal Arch. Cryptic Councils, which are in some places called Councils of Royal and Select Masters, confer 2 degrees: Royal Master and Select Master. The Commandery or Knights Templar confers three Orders. Royal Arch Chapters, Cryptic Councils, and Commanderies each hold meetings just as Lodges do, but with different rituals than Lodges.

MM-24. Can any Mason join the Scottish Rite and the York Rite?

Any mason can petition to join the Scottish

Rite and the York Rite's Royal Arch Chapters and Cryptic (or Royal and Select Masters) Councils. However, the Commandery, or Knights Templar, is restricted to Masons who belong to the Christian faith. Each Mason can choose to join either the Scottish Rite or the York Rite, or both, or neither.

MM-25. How do you decide which to join, if you want to join either?

Talk with Masons who belong to the Scottish Rite and the York Rite, read books about them, and ask questions the same way you did when you were thinking of petitioning to become a Mason.

MM-26. What are other appendant bodies for Masons?

Other groups that require Masonic membership of their applicants include the Shrine, the Grotto, and the Tall Cedars of Lebanon. There are many other Masonic groups that have membership requirements such as having to be invited to join, being a member of one of the other Masonic groups, or belonging to a particular religion. However, it is important to remember, again, that the most important Masonic membership any Mason can ever have is in his Craft, or Blue Lodge, and the most important title for any Mason is that of Master Mason.

MM-27. Are there Masonic appendant bodies or Lodges for women?

The Order of the Eastern Star includes both

women and men among its members; men must be Masons and women members of the Star must be related to a Mason. The Order of the Amaranth is another group that includes Masons and women who are related to Masons. There are also groups that include women who are related to Masons who belong to certain other appendant bodies, such as the Shrine.

There are also Masonic Lodges and Grand Lodges that include only women, and Masonic Lodges and Grand Lodges that include men and women together. Our branch of "mainstream" Freemasonry does not recognize these groups that include women as being a part of Freemasonry as we know it, but it is a fact that there are many thousands of women practicing Freemasonry in most countries that have male Masons, including the U.S.

MM-28. What is meant by (a) recognized and unrecognized Grand Lodges, (b) regular and irregular Masonry, and (c) clandestine Lodges and clandestine Masons?

This can be a very complicated subject. Many people say definite things about "regular" or "clandestine" Grand Lodges, but often what they say is inaccurate and confusing.

The only thing that can be said with complete accuracy about any Grand Lodge is that "My Grand Lodge recognizes that Grand Lodge as of this time" or "My Grand Lodge does not recognize that Grand

Lodge as of this time." Sometimes Grand Lodges that recognize each other are said to be "in amity" with each other.

Some will say that some Grand Lodges are "regular" and others are not, but no one can said with any authority what this means. Some say "regular" means a Grand Lodge that is recognized (but by whom?), some say it is a Grand Lodge that follows the "Ancient Landmarks" (but no one knows what that means because most Grand Lodges have different lists of Landmarks), and some say a Grand Lodge is "regular" when it follows the "Old Charges" (but again, this is not clear to everyone, and in some cases the Old Charges are different from what a Grand Lodge now considers to be Landmarks).

Similarly, some say a Grand Lodge is "irregular" or "clandestine" if it does not have a charter, was not formed "properly," does not require its members to express a belief in God, does not accept men of all religions, or does not follow what some Grand Lodges consider to be "basic" about Freemasonry. However, there is no agreement that any of these "definitions" of these terms is the "true" definition, so terms such as "irregular" or "clandestine" are more confusing than helpful.

If a Grand Lodge is recognized, as of a certain time, by another Grand Lodge, that usually means that members of Lodges in one of these Grand Lodges can visit Lodges in the other Grand Lodge, and vice versa. It also sometimes means that both Grand Lodges appoint "Grand Representatives" to represent each one to the other, and often that some officers of both Grand Lodges attend the meetings of the other Grand Lodge. In many cases, Grand Lodges that recognize each other also allow their members to join Lodges in the other Grand Lodge, but this is not always the case. In some cases Grand Lodge recognize each other but do not allow their members to join any other Lodges except their own.

As you can see, questions about whether a Grand Lodge or a group of Grand Lodges are "regular" or "irregular" or "clandestine" or "recognized" or "unrecognized" are confusing, and it should also be noted that some Masons become very emotional about these subjects.

MM-29. What are Masonic youth groups?

There are several organizations for young people that are supported by Freemasonry. In some of them, it is necessary to be related to, or to be sponsored by, a Mason to join. The International Order of DeMolay is the youth organization for young boys. The International Order of Job's Daughters and the Order of Rainbow for Girls are Masonic-related organizations for young girls. By supporting these groups, Masons help provide youth with important values of morality, and from DeMolay we can often find future Masons.

MM-30. What is the role of the Grand Lodge and the Grand Master?

The Grand Lodge is the supreme authority of Freemasonry in each Grand Jurisdiction. When the Grand Lodge is not in session, the Grand Master has the authority of the Grand Lodge and he usually has the authority to set aside any Masonic law and do anything he feels is necessary for the good of Freemasonry in that jurisdiction. Grand Masters are often called upon to make decisions interpreting the laws of Freemasonry. Each of these Grand Masters' decisions are reviewed by the Grand Lodge each year, and if approved by the Grand Lodge, becomes the continuing law for Freemasonry in that jurisdiction.

MM-31. What are the types of rules established by Grand Lodges, and how can one find these rules?

Examples of these rules are those which set the date and time when the Grand Lodge will meet and how it will conduct its business. Also, how new Lodges can be formed, and what types of reports each Lodge has to file with the Grand Lodge. Other examples of these rules are those which state what a man has to do to petition to become a Mason, and how he progresses from one Degree to the next. Rules established by Grand Lodges are usually compiled in a book called the Code

MM-32. What is the composition of a Grand Lodge?

Each Grand Lodge has different rules about

who are the official members of that Grand Lodge. This is not the same as all the Masons in the Lodges of the Grand Lodge, as many of those Masons are not considered to be "members" of the Grand Lodge in the sense of being allowed to vote or even be present at Grand Lodge meetings.

Grand Lodges are usually composed of the Grand Master, elected Grand Lodge officers, appointed Grand Lodge officers, one or more representatives of each Lodge, and such other officers or members as stated in the Grand Lodge Code.

MM-33. Who are the officers of Grand Lodges?

The elected officers of most U.S. Grand Lodges are the Grand Master, the Deputy Grand Master, the Senior Grand Warden, the Junior Grand Warden, the Grand Treasurer, the Grand Secretary, the Senior Grand Deacon, and the Junior Grand Deacon. The Grand Master usually also appoints several Grand Lodge officers, including the Grand Marshal, Grand Chaplain, Grand Lecturer, Grand Tiler, and others.

MM-34. How does one become a Grand Lodge member or officer?

You have to be elected or appointed. For example, in most Grand Lodges each Lodge has one or more representatives who are official "members" of the Grand Lodge, including at least the Worshipful Master. The Grand Lodge officers who are voting members of the Grand Lodge are elected in accordance with the rules of each Grand Lodge. The Grand Master or others appoint Grand Lodge appointive officers. In most Grand Lodges, once a Mason is appointed or elected into the Grand Lodge "progressive" line, he usually is appointed or elected to the next highest office each year, until he becomes Grand Master. However, in some jurisdictions this is not the case.

MM-35. When do Grand Lodges meet, and what happens at their meetings?

Grand Lodges usually meet at the same time each year. There are usually a number of reports and speeches, plus presentation of proposed resolutions that would change the rules of Freemasonry in that jurisdiction, plus the election and installation of Grand Lodge officers. There are also a number of social events such as banquets.

MM-36. Who can attend Grand Lodge meetings?

In most jurisdictions Masons are encouraged to attend their Grand Lodge meetings. Those who are not voting members can observe what occurs at the tiled meetings of the Grand Lodge. Non-Masons are also welcome at the social events.

MM-37. Who are District Deputy Grand Masters?

Some jurisdictions have Districts, with District Deputy Grand Masters appointed by the Grand Master to represent him in each District. They are usually recommended to the Grand Master by the Lodges in their District. Lodge officers can ask District Deputy Grand Masters for advice, and to relay messages or requests to the Grand Master. When a District Deputy Grand Master speaks on behalf of the Grand Master, it carries the authority of the Grand Master.

MM-38. How are new Lodges started, and how can they be ended?

In most jurisdictions, when Masons wish to form a new Lodge they apply to the Grand Master for a dispensation to permit them to form and work temporarily. If, after a period, this new Lodge has met certain standards, the Grand Lodge may grant it a Charter. The Grand Lodge can revoke a Lodge's charter. Also, in most U.S. jurisdictions the Grand Master can literally pick up a Lodge's charter, and the Lodge then ceases to exist.

MM-39. How are Lodge officers elected?

The rules for election of Lodge officers vary in each jurisdiction, and sometimes within jurisdictions. Sometimes the Worshipful Master conducts elections for the officers for the coming year, sometimes nominations are made, sometimes the members elect their officers by writing names on blank pieces of paper without anyone being nominated, and sometimes other election methods are used.

MM-40. *What are the rules about Masonic visitation?*

Each Mason is permitted to visit his own and other Masonic Lodges, under most circumstances. The Worshipful Master of each Lodge is required to insure that each visitor truly is a Mason, and is in good standing in his Lodge at the time of the requested visit. This can be done by examining the visitor's dues card, and by having some of the members of the Lodge examine the potential visitor by asking him in private to demonstrate the due guards and signs of a Mason, or by otherwise proving his Masonic qualifications. Also, each Lodge should insure that the Lodge to which a visitor belongs is under a Grand Lodge that is recognized by the Grand Lodge that has chartered that Lodge. Each visitor should recognize that it is polite to arrive early enough to allow time for these procedures to be followed, and to give advance notice to the Worshipful Master of a planned visit if that is possible. An easier way to obtain entrance into a Lodge you are visiting is to have one of the members, or someone who has previously visited that Lodge, vouch for the fact that he has sat in another Lodge with you, thus proving that you are a Mason.

MM-41. *Can a visitor be barred from a Lodge meeting?*

In most jurisdictions, if a member of a Lodge objects to any visitor attending that Lodge meeting the Worshipful Master must not permit the visitor to attend that

Lodge meeting. There are exceptions, though. Certain Grand Lodge officers cannot be barred from any Lodge meeting. Also, in some jurisdictions if a Worshipful Master believes that a member of the Lodge is objecting to a visitor because of the race or color of that visiting Mason, the Worshipful Master is required to overrule the objection and permit the visitor to attend the meeting.

This can sometimes be a very touchy subject. In most jurisdictions the Worshipful Master cannot overrule any member who objects to a visitor (with some exceptions, such as the Grand Master), but there are other things that can, and have been done. For example, the Worshipful Master can open and close the Lodge meeting with proper ritual, but then have the program of the meeting conducted after the Lodge is closed but with everyone still present, including the visitor whose presence in the official Lodge meeting was objectionable to one of the Lodge members.

It if often said that objection to a visitor should never be made because of any trivial matter and the teachings of Freemasonry should always be the guide. At all times, the peace and harmony of the Lodge must be preserved, but also the Masonic teachings of morality, tolerance, and equality of all people should be remembered.

MM-42. *How is balloting done in Lodges on potential new members?*

There is a strict ritual about how Lodge members vote on potential new members. After all the preliminary steps have been taken, including reading of a petition from a candidate, investigation, and anything else, a ballot is taken. Each member of the Lodge votes yes or no by placing a white ball or a black cube in a receptacle in the ballot box. After all have voted, the Worshipful Master and Wardens examine the ballot box to see if any black cubes have been cast. Balloting in Lodges on petition-ers is strictly secret. In most jurisdictions, if one black cube is cast the petitioner is rejected, but in England, New York, Texas, and some other jurisdictions, three black cubes are needed to reject a petitioner. In most jurisdictions, too, it is a violation of Masonic law for anyone to reveal or discuss how he voted on a petition.

MM-43. *How is voting done on other issues in Lodges?*

Voting on issues such as who should be elected to each of the officer positions, or whether the Lodge should vote to spend money for an item, or on any other issue, is usually done by raising of hands, or calling out aye or nay.

MM-44. *What dues or other financial obligations does a Mason have?*

Each Lodge has dues set by the Lodge, and each Mason must pay these dues to remain in good standing. If he cannot pay his dues because of financial hardship, he should speak privately with the Worshipful Master, and the Lodge may waive his dues, meaning allow him to remain a member without paying dues for the time being. If a Mason does not pay his dues, and does not respond to requests from the Lodge, he may be suspended for non-payment of dues and he will no longer be in good standing and thus no longer allowed to attend any Lodges in most jurisdictions. Grand Lodges also require each Lodge to pay a certain amount to the Grand Lodge based on the number of members in each Lodge. To the extent he is able, each Mason also should help by voluntarily contributing to Masonic charities and helping fellow Masons and their families who may be in need.

MM-45. Can a Mason resign from his Lodge, or join another Lodge?

A Mason can leave his Lodge by requesting a demit, which means a document certifying that at the time he left his Lodge he was in good standing financially and not under Masonic charges. A demitted Mason can apply to rejoin that, or any other Lodge, but must be accepted by ballot of the Lodge. Usually, a member of one Lodge can join another without demitting from the first Lodge. He simply applies for affiliation or membership in the second, or third, etc., Lodge, and if accepted he is a member of as many Lodges as he wishes and as will have him. Masons should be aware, though, that in some states Masons are allowed to belong to only one or two Lodges.

MM-46. What happens if a member of more than one Lodge is suspended for not paying his dues to one of them?

If a Mason is suspended from one Lodge, he will be suspended from all Lodges, and from all appendant bodies. That is why each Mason should keep up with all his obligations, or else ask for a demit from any Lodge in which he no longer wants to hold membership.

MM-47. Can Masons be suspended or expelled?

A Mason can be accused of un-Masonic conduct, and if found guilty, he can be reprimanded, suspended, or expelled. Grand Lodges have rules to be followed to handle allegations of un-Masonic conduct and to conduct trials on these charges in a manner that is fair to all concerned. It is very important that Masons understand that everyone should be assumed to be innocent, regardless of what you might hear or how things may appear, unless and until evidence is presented, the accused person has a fair opportunity to defend himself, and an objective decision is reached.

MM-48. What is the staff of a Grand Lodge, where are they, and what do they do?

Grand Lodge staffs are located in the headquarters of each Grand Lodge. The staff is headed by the Grand Secretary of the jurisdiction, who is elected by the Grand Lodge. Grand Lodge staff handles the record-keeping of tracking all the Lodges in their jurisdictions, plus all the members of each Lodge: who has paid dues, who has moved, who has died, etc. Grand Lodge staffs also sell publications about Freemasonry, and in other ways try to assist Lodges and their officers and members. Many Grand Lodge offices also include libraries and museums. Masons are encouraged to visit them.

MM-49. What is a Masonic Home?

Many Grand Lodges maintain retirement homes for their members and their families. They provide homes for their older Masons, their wives and widows.

MM-50. What is Prince Hall Freemasonry?

In 1775, an African-American man named Prince Hall was made a Mason, together with fourteen other African-Americans, in a Lodge in Boston that was operating under a charter issued by the Grand Lodge of Ireland. In 1784 Prince Hall and his Brethren received a charter issued by the Grand Lodge of England, and later, in memory of their founder, all of the Masonic Lodges for African-Americans came to be called Prince Hall Masonry. With some up's and down's during the years, Freemasonry for African-American men has prospered in the United States and it has Grand Lodges and Masonic Lodges in all parts of our country and in some foreign countries, too. Until recently, our branch of Freemasonry did not recognize Prince Hall Masonry, but starting in 1989 many Grand Lodges started recognizing Prince Hall Grand Lodges and allowing visits of Masons between our two systems. As of 2005, three-quarters of all the Grand Lodges in the United States (38 out of 51) recognize Prince Hall Masonry, as well as all the Grand Lodges in Canada, plus England, and other countries.

MM-51. Do Prince Hall Masons do the same thing that we do in our Lodges?

Yes. They confer the Degrees in almost the same way we do, have similar Lodge arrangements and officers, Grand Lodges, and appendant bodies just as our branch of Masonry does.

MM-52. What is meant by "profane"?

That is an archaic term formerly used to refer to someone who was not a Mason. It never meant someone who used profanity, or who was not a good person, but it is usually considered an insult to call someone a profane so this term should not be used. Someone who is not a Mason can more politely be referred to as a non-Mason.

MM-53. What is Masonic relief?

Each Mason is obliged to do whatever he can to assist Masonic Brethren who are in need, and any Mason may apply for

Masonic relief when he is in need. Each individual, each Lodge, and each Grand Lodge may determine what is appropriate to do in each case. Widows and orphans of Freemasons also are permitted to apply for Masonic relief if it is needed.

MM-54. What are Masonic funeral services?

Each Masonic jurisdiction has a ritual that is used when the Brethren pay their respects to a Mason who has died. This ritual can be performed in public, either at the funeral home or at the grave site. It is up to the family of the departed Mason to request a Lodge to perform a Masonic funeral service, so each Mason should inform his family ahead of time if he would like them to make this request after his death.

MM-55. What is antimasonry and who is opposed to Freemasonry?

As long as Freemasonry has existed, there have been some who oppose it. Some oppose it because Freemasonry supports freedom and democracy, and not everyone supports those ideals. Some oppose it because Freemasonry welcomes men of all religions, and some antimasons feel only those of their religion should be accepted in any organization. Some feel that Freemasonry has at times been too powerful, or are upset by some of the aspects of the ritual that have become known to the public. Some may become antimasons just because they feel they can make money by producing antimasonic books and videotapes, or appearing on antimasonic television programs. Often, those who oppose Freemasonry do so because they do not have the facts about what Masons do and what our organization represents.

MM-56. Was there really a political party in the United States that was opposed to Freemasonry?

Yes. In the 1820's through the 1840's a large group of people came to feel that Freemasonry was a bad influence in America. They founded an official political party called the Antimasonic Party, which achieved some successes in electing members of Congress, state Governors, and other public officials. This party started after it was claimed in 1826 that a man named William Morgan had been kidnaped and possibly murdered by Masons in northern New York state because he was threatening to write a book disclosing the secrets of Freemasonry. No one knows for sure what happened to Morgan. What is certain is that many people came to feel that Masons tried to help Brother Masons in ways that were contrary to law and the democratic ideals of America. This led to successes for the Antimasonic Party in the New England states, New York, and Pennsylvania. Freemasonry was severely damaged in America during this period, but it was built up again starting in the 1840s.

MM-57. Are there still people who oppose Freemasonry?

Yes. Some people continue to oppose Freemasonry. Some believe, incorrectly, that Masonry is a religion in competition with other religions. Some believe, completely incorrectly, that Freemasonry promotes devil worship. Some believe stories that Freemasonry attempts to take over the world and overthrow governments. Some are opposed to an organization that teaches tolerance, democracy, and freedom. Just because some people make allegations against Freemasonry, and even though the allegations are repeated, it does not mean that there is any truth in them.

MM-58. Why have totalitarian regimes attacked Freemasonry?

Hitler ordered Freemasonry abolished in Nazi Germany. Mussolini jailed Freemasons in Fascist Italy, as did Franco in Fascist Spain. Stalin also banned Freemasonry in the Communist Soviet Union, and Freemasonry was prohibited in Communist countries in general, and in Iran, since the revolution of the Ayatollah Khomeini. Freemasonry is banned and Masons are sometimes jailed because Masonry supports democracy and freedom, or because some view it as allied with the Western world or with Judaism.

MM-59. Are there any religions that oppose Freemasonry?

Some people, who at some times have been leaders of certain religions, have opposed

Freemasonry. For many years the Catholic Church, through the Popes, prohibited its members from becoming Masons (although many of them joined anyway). Since the 1980's the automatic excommunication of any Catholics who become Masons was eliminated. There have also been some efforts in the Baptist Church, and parts of the Lutheran Church, to oppose Freemasonry, and there have been some disputes between the LDS Church (Mormons) and Freemasonry. Rev. Pat Robertson and some others strongly oppose Freemasonry now. Many of these disputes were the results of misunderstandings or misinformation, or opposition to the strong policy of Freemasonry of accepting and tolerating men of all religions.

MM-60. Are Masons permitted to wear Masonic jewelry or symbols in public?

Yes. Each Mason can decide for himself whether or not he wishes to wear Masonic jewelry, Masonic signs on his car, or to display his Masonic membership or not. Many Masons in the United States do display their membership proudly, but Masons in other countries usually consider it bad taste to display their Masonic membership in public.

MM-61. When is a man truly a Mason?

After a man receives the Entered Apprentice Degree, we tell him he is a Mason, and after he receives the Master Mason Degree he is a full member of his Lodge. But in a larger sense, no man ever truly becomes a Master Mason because our ritual teaches that we are always striving to improve our characters and our actions toward our fellow men, to receive more divine guidance, and to help make society a better place for everyone. Each man works his whole life to be a better man and to help others. That is how each of us may finally and truly become a Mason.

MM-62. What are some books Master Masons can read to learn more about Freemasonry?

The Grand Design
by Wallace McLeod, published in 1991

Let Your Work Become Your Mark
by Stewart W. Miner, published in 1986

The Master's Book
by Carl H. Claudy, published in 1935

Key to Freemasonry's Growth
by Allen E. Roberts, published in 1969

101+ Ways to Improve Interest & Attendance in Your Masonic Lodge
by the Masonic Renewal Committee of North America, Inc.

Is It True What They Say About Freemasonry?
by Art deHoyos & S. Brent Morris, 2nd edition published in 1997

A Pilgrim's Path: One Man's Road to the Masonic Temple
by John J. Robinson, published in 1993

Coil's Masonic Encyclopedia
by Henry W. Coil, 2nd edition by Allen E. Roberts published in 1996

Living the Enlightenment: Freemasonry and Politics in Eighteenth-Century Europe
by Margaret C. Jacob, published in 1991

Revolutionary Brotherhood: Freemasonry and the Transformation of the American Social Order, 1730-1840
by Steven Bullock, published in 1996

Appendixes

Appendix A
"Definitions" of Freemasonry

There is no single, "official" definition of Freemasonry. In fact, there is no single or "official" leader or ruling body of Freemasonry. In the United States, in each state there are one or more Grand Lodges, each of which can define Freemasonry any way it wishes, and the same is true in most countries in the world. Many Grand Lodges do not even define Freemasonry, but allow each of their members to define Freemasonry any way they wish.

Here is a definition of Freemasonry that I think is appropriate:

Freemasonry is an organization whose goals include:

1. Helping its members improve themselves through education and improved knowledge of themselves and others.

2. Brotherhood of all people and tolerance of differences among people.

3. Support of democracy, freedom, individual rights, and the dignity of all people.

4. Mutual assistance, including helping fellow members' families.

5. Charity and assistance to the community, especially those in need.

Some Masonic writers and researchers have written their own definitions of Freemasonry.

William Preston said Freemasonry's role is spreading knowledge. Masons should study and learn more about all subjects. Another idea is that Freemasonry's purpose is the perfection of humanity by organizing the moral sentiments of mankind, improving law and government. George Oliver felt Freemasonry is best understood in relation to the philosophy of religion, as a means for us to know God and his works, by handing down tradition. Albert Pike said that Freemasonry is a method of studying basic principles and its goal is to reveal and give us possession of the universal principle by which we may master the universe, the Absolute. We should study the allegories and symbols of Freemasonry until they reveal the light to each of us individually.

Roscoe Pound and others in the early 1900's talked about a modern approach, that Freemasonry's goal is to preserve, develop, and transmit to posterity the civilization passed on to us, by insisting on the universality of mankind and the transmission of an immemorial tradition of human solidarity. William E. Hammond talked of moral discipline, where Masonry produces the finest type of character and culture through fellowship and mutual helpfulness. Joseph Fort Newton said Freemasonry is a form of public service and public mindedness. We have a social duty to help our neighbors by work in our communities, to promote the freedoms of the mind unhampered by dictation by anyone, with education for all to maintain democracy, and to unite people in common service for mankind.

Allen E. Roberts and Albert Mackey said Masonry is a system of ethics and brotherhood, making men better not just to themselves but to each other. It teaches the meaning of life and death, with the search for the lost word, the attempt to find God's truth in our lives. We should act towards others as we want them to act towards us, with faith in the social, eternal, and intellectual progress of mankind.

Arthur E. Waite and W.L. Wilmshurst wrote about Masonry as essentially a spiritual activity. Waite described it as the mysticism of a first-hand experience with God, with symbols for those who are not yet capable of understanding. Wilmshurst talked of spiritual life as the meaning of the Masonic ritual and symbols, all leading toward a path of life higher than we normally tread, an inner world where the ancient mysteries of our being are to be learned. J.S.M. Ward described Freemasonry as combining ideals — political, social, ritualistic, archeological, historical, and mystical into the "great" idea. W. Kirk MacNulty described Freemasonry as a method to learn more about our own minds, and to transform our being to a higher plane where we are reborn in a higher state. He used recent understanding of the psychological needs of all people to explain the role of Freemasonry in the life of every Mason.

H.L. Haywood said Freemasonry is a system of ethics, showing each man the way toward a new birth of his nature as symbolized in the Hiram Abif drama, bringing divine power to bear on each individual. The great teachings of Freemasonry are equality, which is synonymous with Masonry, meaning the equal right of all people to use our own minds and abilities; liberty, meaning the unhindered full exercise of our nature and mind; and the right of people to govern themselves, even if they sometimes make mistakes. He was optimistic about the human ability to improve through education, to enrich human life with the human family living happily together.

Henry Wilson Coil, in *Coil's Encyclopedia of Freemasonry*, (Macoy Publishing, Richmond, Virginia, 1961, revised edition 1995, pages 164-165) listed definitions of Freemasonry in different categories:

Definition of Freemasonry in all times and places:

Freemasonry is an oath-bound fraternal order of men; deriving from the medieval fraternity of operative Freemasons; adhering to many of their Ancient Charges, laws, customs, and legends; loyal to the civil government under which it exists; inculcating moral and social virtues by symbolic application of the working tools of the stonemasons and by allegories, lectures, and charges; the members of which are obligated to observe principles of brotherly love, equality, mutual aid and assistance, secrecy, and confidence; have secret modes of recognizing one another as Masons when abroad in the world; and meet in lodges, each governed somewhat autocratically by a Master, assisted by Wardens, where petitioners, after particular enquiry into their mental, moral and physical qualifications, are formally admitted into the Society in secret ceremonies based in part on old legends of the Craft.

Every Masonic lodge in existence or that ever has existed, so far as known, answers that description; no other order that exists or ever has existed does so.

Definition of Modern Craft Masonry, supplementing the above definition:

In modern times, the Fraternity has spread over the civilized portions of the globe and has experienced some mutations in its organization, doctrine, and practices, so that lodges have come to be subordinate to, or constituent of, Grand Lodges presided over by Grand Masters, each sovereign within a given nation, state, or other political subdivision, and there is generally, though not universally, inculcated in, and demanded of the candidate, who ordinarily seeks admission of his own free will and accord, a belief in a Supreme Being and, less generally, in immortality of the soul, the Holy Bible or other Volume of Sacred Law being displayed in the lodge and used for the obligation of the candidate during his course through the three degrees of Entered Apprentice, Fellow Craft, and Master Mason, the last including the legend of King Solomon's Temple and Hiram Abif, though additional degrees and ceremonies are not found objectionable in some jurisdictions.

Definition of Freemasonry in its broadest sense:

Freemasonry, in its broadest and most comprehensive sense, is a system of morality and social ethics, and a philosophy of life, all of simple and fundamental character, incorporating a broad humanitarianism and, though treating life as a practical experience, subordinates the material to the spiritual; it is of no sect but finding truth in all; it is moral but not pharisaic; it demands sanity rather than sanctity; it is tolerant but not supine; it seeks truth but does not define truth; it urges it votaries to think but does not tell them what to think; it despises ignorance but does not proscribe the ignorant; it fosters education but proposes no curriculum; it espouses political liberty and the dignity of man but has no platform or propaganda; it believes in the nobility and usefulness of life; it is modest and not militant; it is moderate, universal, and so liberal as to permit each individual to form and express his own opinion, even as to what Freemasonry is or ought to be, and invites him to improve it if he can.

Freemasonry is a Fraternity composed of moral men of legal age who believe in God and, of their own free will, receive in lodges degrees which depict a system of morality that, as they grow in maturity, teaches them to be tolerant of the beliefs of others, to be patriotic, law-abiding, temperate in all things, to aid the unfortunate, to practice Brotherly Love, and to faithfully accept and discharge solemn obligations.

It is governed by a Grand Lodge which is composed of Grand Officers and representatives of all of the regular lodges within its Jurisdiction, and selects a Grand Master periodically to rule over the organization within the framework of the Constitutions of Freemasonry as adapted for its particular needs.

In short, Freemasonry is a way of life. As an organization, its purpose is to make good men better.

Appendix B
Masonic Dating Systems

Masonic Group: Common practice
Abbreviation: A.D.
Full Name: Anno Domini
Translation: Year of Our Lord
How Computed: current year
Rationale: Said to date from the birth of Jesus Christ (which actually probably took place around 4 B.C.)

Masonic Group: Craft Lodges ("basic" Freemasonry)
Abbreviation: A.L.
Full Name: Anno Lucis
Translation: Year of Light
How Computed: add 4,000 to current year
Rationale: It is said that Bishop Usher in 1611 computed that date the world began as 4,000 B.C. (actually he said 4,004 B.C.)

Masonic Group: Royal Arch Freemasonry
Abbreviation: A. Inv.
Full Name: Anno Inventionis
Translation: Year of the Discovery
How Computed: add 530 to current year
Rationale: The 2nd Temple in Jerusalem was begun in 530 B.C., and it is said that certain items were discovered then.

Masonic Group: Cryptic Masonry Royal & Select Masters
Abbreviation: A. Dep.
Full Name: Anno Depositionis
Translation: Year of the Deposit
How Computed: add 1,000 to current year
Rationale: King Solomon's Temple is said to have been completed in 1,000 B.C., and certain items are said to have been deposited then.

Masonic Group: Knights Templar Commandery
Abbreviation: A.O.
Full Name: Anno Ordinis
Translation: Year of the Order
How Computed: subtract 1,118 from current year
Rationale: The medieval Knights Templar Order was founded in 1118 A.D.

Masonic Group: Scottish Rite
Abbreviation: A.M.
Full Name: Anno Mundi
Translation: Year of the World
How Computed: until Sept. add 3,759 to current year, after Sept. add 3,760 to current year
Rationale: Same as the Hebrew calendar, from the supposed creation of the world in 3760 B.C.

Masonic Group: Order of High Priesthood
Abbreviation: A.B.
Full Name: Anno Benefacionis
Translation: Year of Blessing
How Computed: add 1,913 to current year
Rationale: Abraham is said to have been blessed by the High Priest Melchizedek in 1913 B.C.

Masonic Group: Holy Royal Arch Knight Templar Priests
Abbreviation: A.R.
Full Name: Anno Renascent
Translation: Year of Revival
How Computed: subtract 1,686 from current year
Rationale: This Order is said to have been revived in 1686 A.D.

Appendix C
Masonic Communications Using Computers
e-groups and lists on the internet
Description (taken from the website of each email group)
Who is in charge
How to Subscribe and Unsubscribe
How to post messages (if you are "subscribed")

Antients - yahoogroup
Freemasons preserving antient traditions is an email group set up by a brother in Australia who would like to see many of the older masonic ways - rituals and ceremonial traditions - returned to and ceremonies performed in true and antient form (if such a thing exists!). This offers us a chance to discuss alternative rituals, rites and ceremonies within the bounds of our obligations of course. Perhaps we can get into just what is an "antient landmark" and what is an "innovation" too. This is not to stifle progress, or the enlightenment of truth, but to encourage a look at changes that have occurred and those which have not occurred, and to ask why - and how freemasonry can remain both relevant to society and in touch with its deeper meanings and purposes.
Group Moderator: antients-owner@egroups.com
To subscribe: send a message to
antients-subscribe@egroups.com or go the this e-group's home page at: http://www.egroups.com/list/antients
Members (as of September 2005): 148
Founded: Nov 5, 1998
Post message: antients@yahoogroups.com
Subscribe: antients-subscribe@yahoogroups.com
Unsubscribe: antients-unsubscribe@yahoogroups.com
List owner: antients-owner@yahoogroups.com

Blue-Light - yahoogroup
This group is designed to address any and all issues pertaining to Freemasonry and/or Chapters of OES. It is also to provide Masons from around the world a forum to discuss their con-

cerns, and to get a better understanding of what it is to be a Freemason or Eastern Star. Its aim is to unite in harmony with all races and to tolerate all Religions and Beliefs no matter what their culture might be. Conversations do not have to be about Freemasonary but of any concern or discussion one feels is of interest as long it is a respectful one.
Members (as of September 2005): 141
Founded: Aug 25, 2001
Post message: BLUE_@yahoogroups.com
Subscribe: BLUE_-subscribe@yahoogroups.com
Unsubscribe: BLUE_-unsubscribe@yahoogroups.com
List owner: BLUE_-owner@yahoogroups.com
Owner & Moderator: Ezekiel MuAkil Bey

FM-Reforms - yahoogroup
International network for discussion and researching for practical modes and steps towards a universal fraternity.
Members (as of September 2005): 81
Founded: Feb 27, 2001
Post message: FM-Reforms@yahoogroups.co.uk
Subscribe: FM-Reforms-subscribe@yahoogroups.co.uk
Unsubscribe: FM-Reforms-unsubscribe@yahoogroups.co.uk
List owner: FM-Reforms-owner@yahoogroups.co.uk

Freemason - yahoogroup
This is a forum for Freemasons and lovers of the craft to express ideas and opinions on such subjects that may be of interest to Masonry in general, or to an individual or lodge in particular.
Members (as of September 2005): 566
Founded: Sep 23, 1998
Post message: freemason@yahoogroups.com
Subscribe: freemason-subscribe@yahoogroups.com
Unsubscribe: freemason-unsubscribe@yahoogroups.com
List owner: freemason-owner@yahoogroups.com
Owner & Moderator: Geoffrey Allan
Other Moderator: Tim Gatewood

Freemasons - yahoogroup
Freemasons and appendant body members are welcome here to discuss Freemasonry in a civilized manner. Non Masons are welcome too.
Members (as of September 2005): 273
Founded: Feb 4, 1999
Post message: freemasons@yahoogroups.com
Subscribe: freemasons-subscribe@yahoogroups.com
Unsubscribe: freemasons-unsubscribe@yahoogroups.com
List owner: freemasons-owner@yahoogroups.com

Freemasonry - yahoogroup
Worldwide e-mail group of freemasonry to research and culture exchange.
Group Moderator: freemasonry-owner@egroups.com
To subscribe, send a message to egroups.com-subscribe@freemasonry
Members (as of September 2005): 210
Founded: Oct 2, 1998
Related Link: http://www.ostemplarios.org.br
Post message: freemasonry@yahoogroups.com
Subscribe: freemasonry-subscribe@yahoogroups.com
Unsubscribe: freemasonry-unsubscribe@yahoogroups.com
List owner: freemasonry-owner@yahoogroups.com

Freemasonry for the Next Generation - yahoogroup
This is an international forum to discuss Freemasonry sponsored by Freemasonry for The Next Generation , the Independent e-Zine for the Free-Thinking Freemasonry.
Members (as of September 2005): 188
Founded: Jun 4, 2004
Related Link: http://www.phmainstreet.com/flmason/
Post message: freemasons4_ng@yahoogroups.com
Subscribe: freemasons4_ng-subscribe@yahoogroups.com
Unsubscribe: freemasons4_ng-unsubscribe@yahoogroups.com
List owner: freemasons4_ng-owner@yahoogroups.com

Free-Mason - yahoogroup
The Universal E-Mail Group of Freemasonry is an english language international forum for Freemasons and Lovers of The
Craft who share similar interests in Freemasonry to: * share
masonic research, * exchange masonic culture and freemasonry
information, * express ideas and opinions on masonic subjects
that may be of interest to Freemasonry in general. Brothers,
please keep in mind that this is an open-to-all forum and not a
tyled lodge. Non-masons are welcome and encouraged, regardless of religion or gender as well, whose aim is to improve
his/her knowledge of masonic issues, as well as for providing
a better familiarity with the purposes of the Universal Freemasonry, to discuss and possibly enhance them, and also to allow
for a better acquaintance among persons who have some interest in the subject. The name of the list is free-mason to mean that
freemasonry is the topic no matter what country, perspective or
obedience, as long as: You're respectful of differences (that is:
disagree if necessary but don't disdain); You're on topic (that is:
no discussion on for e.g. politics or religion if it carries no direct
reference to freemasonry); You don't send commercials or brief
messages whose contents is limited to web addresses (that is:
no spam, web link, ad, one-liner, etc.); You use the "English"
language (that is: no posts in any other language)
Members (as of September 2005): 681
Founded: Jul 13, 1999
Related Link: mailto:Free-Mason-Owner@yahoogroups.com
Post message: Free-Mason@yahoogroups.com
Subscribe: Free-Mason-subscribe@yahoogroups.com
Unsubscribe: Free-Mason-unsubscribe@yahoogroups.com
List owner: Free-Mason-owner@yahoogroups.com

Free-Masonry - yahoogroup
This is an english/american english language list and it is meant
to help people who share interests in FreeMasonry. Archives
prior to november 2000 can be found on this list's website. Since
november 1, 2000 archives are available also on the yahoogroups
space. Please note that this list is not restricted to people di-

rectly involved with Free-Masonry or involved with a specific Obedience, but is available for any person, regardless of religion or gender as well, whose aim is to improve his/her knowledge of masonic issues, as well as for providing a better familiarity with the purposes of the Universal Freemasonry, to discuss and possibly enhance them, and also to allow for a better acquaintance among persons who have some interest in the subject. The name of the list is free-masonry to mean that free-masonry is the topic no matter what perspective or Obedience, as long as: You're respectful of differences (that is: disagree if necessary but don't disdain) You're on topic (that is: no discussion on, say, philosophy or politics or religion if it carries no direct reference to freemasonry) Do not send commercials. Also brief messages whose contents is limited to web addresses cannot be accepted: if everybody would do so any list would soon become a bulk of ads or pseudo-ads and it is implied that who subscribes a list is eager to discuss, not to get one's inbox clustered with futile messages. Also, if Your concept is that FreeMasonry must be enshrouded in deep secrecy, than it is useless to subscribe to a list whose aim is communication.
Members (as of September 2005): 692
Founded: Oct 1, 1998
Related Link:
http://www.unitedscripters.com/hotvamps/masonlink.html
Post message: Free-Masonry@yahoogroups.com
Subscribe: Free-Masonry-subscribe@yahoogroups.com
Unsubscribe: Free-Masonry-unsubscribe@yahoogroups.com
List owner: Free-Masonry-owner@yahoogroups.com

Globalmason - yahoogroup
This is an international forum to discuss Freemasonry.The web site is restricted to MM's from recognized Grand Lodge Jurisdictions and allows a location for chat, e-mail, files, documents, esoteric and exoteric discussions. Membership is offered once a questionnaire is completed and possible contact made to the respective Grand Lodge for current MM standing. The views expressed here are not representative of any recognized Grand

Lodge but of an individual nature. The Global Mason Network Administrative Staff reserve the right to maintain peace and harmony on this web site. Finally, Any Political and Religious Discussions Are Strictly Prohibited. However, it may be necessary to talk about such institutions where Freemasonry is under attack. Topics range from Masonic history, philosophies, origins, archaeology and spirituality to important local lodge issues like candidate instruction, masonic education programs, and ways to improve our lodges and its members.

Members (as of September 2005): 178
Founded: Sep 17, 2002
http://groups.yahoo.com/group/globalmason
Post message: globalmason@yahoogroups.com
Subscribe: globalmason-subscribe@yahoogroups.com
Unsubscribe: globalmason-unsubscribe@yahoogroups.com
List owner: globalmason-owner@yahoogroups.com
Owner & Moderator: Uwe Riches
Other Moderators: Fred Zacher, L. Katz

Kofu33 -Knights of Freemasonry Universal - yahoogroup
Masonic, General Disscussion Open Forum,
Knights of Freemasonry Universal
Members: 116
Founded: Nov 4, 2000
Related Link: http://www.kofu33.org
Post message: kofu33@yahoogroups.com
Subscribe: kofu33-subscribe@yahoogroups.com
Unsubscribe: kofu33-unsubscribe@yahoogroups.com
List owner: kofu33-owner@yahoogroups.com

The Lost Word - yahoogroup
The Lost Word is a Masonic education list for Masons and non-Masons. It is a home for the weary traveler of any path. It is a place for open-minded Masons and non-Masons to grow and experience Masonry as full as possible outside of a lodge. While matters reserved for the lodge are not allowed on the list, the wide Masonic experience permitted for all is encouraged. Mat-

ters of history, symbolism, philosophy, architecture as well as the arts and sciences are open for exploration on this list. Also invited is light chat and lodge/grand lodge announcements. The simple goal is Masonic education in a stimulating environment.

Members (as of September 2005): 354
Founded: Jun 21, 2005
Related Links: http://www.lostword.com and http://www.lostword.info
Post message: thelostword@yahoogroups.com
Subscribe: thelostword-subscribe@yahoogroups.com
Unsubscribe: thelostword-unsubscribe@yahoogroups.com
List owner: thelostword-owner@yahoogroups.com
Owner & Moderator: Michael Poll
Other Moderators: Matt Byers, William R. Cline Jr., David Catten, Keith Duncan, Jim Harvey, John M. Karnes

MasEd - Masonic Education - yahoogroup
This email message exchange group is for those interested in Masonic education. What should Masonic education consist of, what are good ways to promote and conduct Masonic education, what methods have worked or not worked, what are useful tools, etc.? The specific purpose of the MasEd egroup is for those interested in Masonic education to share messages about how to educate Masons; not to be a general Masonic message board. It is to help us all learn how to be better teachers of Freemasonry. This egroup is open to all those who are interested in Masonic education.

Members (as of September 2005): 784
Founded: Jul 17, 2000
Post message: mased@yahoogroups.com
Subscribe: mased-subscribe@yahoogroups.com
Unsubscribe: mased-unsubscribe@yahoogroups.com
List owner: mased-owner@yahoogroups.com
Owner & Moderator: Paul M. Bessel

Mason - yahoogroup
Dedicated to improve the international masonic relationship, making better the communications between members and Lodges also increasing the study of the secret knowledge. Subscribers request will be approved by the moderator. Please, in your e-mail to join, write some words or a setence to confirm that you are a mason including the name and number of your Mother Lodge. Joining this group you are able to write in ENGLISH, PORTUGUESE or SPANISH.
Group Moderator: mason-owner@egroups.com
To subscribe, send a message to egroups.com-subscribe@mason or go the this e-group's home page at
http://www.egroups.com/list/mason
Members (as of September 2005): 186
Founded: Oct 11, 1998
Post message: mason@yahoogroups.com
Subscribe: mason-subscribe@yahoogroups.com
Unsubscribe: mason-unsubscribe@yahoogroups.com
List owner: mason-owner@yahoogroups.com
Moderator: Marcelo Rezende

Masonic - yahoogroup
Members (as of September 2005): 150
Founded: Sep 23, 2001
Post message: Masonic@yahoogroups.com
Subscribe: Masonic-subscribe@yahoogroups.com
Unsubscribe: Masonic-unsubscribe@yahoogroups.com
List owner: Masonic-owner@yahoogroups.com
Owner & Moderator: Frank Hinshaw

Masonic Light - yahoogroup
For open-minded Men and Women Freemasons only, the busy 'masoniclight' YahooGroup discusses all aspects of Freemasonry from the personal perspectives of its member Freemasons from around the globe in a fast-paced respectful manner. Topics range from Masonic history, philosophies, origins, archaeology and spirituality to important local lodge issues like

candidate instruction, masonic education programs, special events and ways to improve our lodges and its members, at an individual and institutional level, in knowledge of all aspects of the Craft, its appendant bodies and other recognized and non-recognized Orders. Rosslyn Chapel is of special interest to our group as well. Men and Women Freemasons from all Masonic Jurisdictions around the earth are welcome to participate in this forum. Visit http://www.masoniclight.org/subscribe.html to enroll!

Members (as of September 2005): 752
Founded: May 8, 2000
Related Link: http://www.masoniclight.org
Post message: masoniclight@yahoogroups.com
Subscribe: masoniclight-subscribe@yahoogroups.com
Unsubscribe: masoniclight-unsubscribe@yahoogroups.com
List owner: masoniclight-owner@yahoogroups.com
Owner & Moderator: Josh Heller

Masonic Pagans - yahoogroup
A list for those interested in both masonry and paganism.
Members (as of September 2005): 119
Founded: May 16, 2000
Post message: Masonic_Pagans@yahoogroups.com
Subscribe: Masonic_Pagans-subscribe@yahoogroups.com
Unsubscribe: Masonic_Pagans-unsubscribe@yahoogroups.com
List owner: Masonic_Pagans-owner@yahoogroups.com

Masonic Research - yahoogroup
This is the right place to talk about research on various Masonic aspects, such as history, Masonry and arts, philosophy and symbolism. Both Masons and non-Masons are heartily welcome. Please do visit the Masonic Research Site.
Members (as of September 2005): 211
Founded: Apr 5, 2001
Related Link: http://www.masonicresearch.de
Post message: masonicresearch@yahoogroups.com
Subscribe: masonicresearch-subscribe@yahoogroups.com

Unsubscribe: masonicresearch-unsubscribe@yahoogroups.com
List owner: masonicresearch-owner@yahoogroups.com
Owner & Moderator: Daniel Hoehr

Masonic Roots - yahoogroup
Masonic Roots group is dedicated to the study of the claim that free masonry dates earlier than 1717, the year of establishing the Premier Grand Lodge in London. All people, masons and non-masons alike, who are interested in this area of history are invited to join and share opinions and documents, or just to lurk. Chapters from Bernard Springett "secret sects" published in 1923 (currently out of print) are available in the files section. Arguments that proof or disproof the link between freemasonry and Knights Templars, Rosicrucioners, Egyptian Rites, and esoteric masonry are welcomed. "Wo him he who knows and does not teach what he knows" – John the Baptist (from a Mandaean text)
Members (as of September 2005): 84
Founded: Oct 7, 2001
Post message: mroots@yahoogroups.com
Subscribe: mroots-subscribe@yahoogroups.com
Unsubscribe: mroots-unsubscribe@yahoogroups.com
List owner: mroots-owner@yahoogroups.com
Owner & Moderator: Bassam Ramez Dagher
Other Moderator: Andy Robertson

Masons Online - yahoogroup
Remember This is not a tyled Lodge...There are many different types of Masons including some who may not be recognized by your Grand Lodge and who may belong to this group. We also have several NON-Masons who are just interested in Masonry. Remember, Watch what you post you never know where you may see it again. Welcome and enjoy the GENERAL discussions. S & F Always, Sylvester C. Spinetta III, 32* MPS, GLoNY Great Kills Lodge No. 912, Amara Shrine Florida
Members (as of September 2005): 232
Founded: Apr 17, 2002

Post message: Masons_Online@yahoogroups.com
Subscribe: Masons_Online-subscribe@yahoogroups.com
Unsubscribe: Masons_Online-unsubscribe@yahoogroups.com
List owner: Masons_Online-owner@yahoogroups.com

MasRec - Masonic Recognition - yahoogroup
This group is for the exchange of information about Masonic recognitions — Recognitions by each Masonic Grand Lodge of other Masonic Grand Lodges — what standards are used, which Grand Lodge is recognized by which other Grand Lodges, what standards are used by each Grand Lodge to make decisions about recognitions of other Grand Lodges, who is involved in recognition decisions in each Grand Lodge, what is the role of the Commission on Information for Recognition of the Conference of Grand Masters of Masons in North America, etc.
Members (as of September 2005): 140
Founded: Jul 23, 2001
Post message: masrec@yahoogroups.com
Subscribe: masrec-subscribe@yahoogroups.com
Unsubscribe: masrec-unsubscribe@yahoogroups.com
List owner: masrec-owner@yahoogroups.com
Owner & Moderator: Paul M. Bessel

MLMA - Masonic Library and Museum Association - yahoogroup
This is the place to find announcements about the Masonic Library & Museum Association. It is also the place to post or read messages by and about the members of the MLMA, and about Masonic libraries and museums. To subscribe, if you are an MLMA member, send a message to paul@bessel.org or go the this group's home page at http://www.yahoogroups.com/mlma
Members (as of September 2005): 82
Founded: Nov 24, 2001
Related Link: http://bessel.org/mlma/
Post message: mlma@yahoogroups.com
Subscribe: mlma-subscribe@yahoogroups.com

Unsubscribe: mlma-unsubscribe@yahoogroups.com
List owner: mlma-owner@yahoogroups.com
Owner & Moderator: Paul M. Bessel
Other Moderator: Glenys Waldman

PHA Research - yahoogroup
Prince Hall Freemasonry Research List. The oldest Prince Hall E-List on the Internet. This Mailing List is for members of the Prince Hall Masonic Family, to discuss Ritualistic, Protocol, History, Symbolic matters relevant to to Prince Hall Freemasonry and Universal Freemasonry. This list is open to Freemasons and Eastern Stars of any Affiliation and Jurisdiction. Our archive and knowledgable list members make the Prince Hall Research E-Group the Premier Universal Research List of Prince Hall Freemasonry. Again - the Primary Object of this List is Masonic Research. Useful books for further reading about Prince Hall Freemasonry: "Black Square and Compass" by Joseph A Walkes, Jr; and "Inside Prince Hall" by David L Gray. Also see http://groups.yahoo.com/group/pharesearch/files/Brother-Prince-Hall/
Members (as of September 2005): 733
Founded: Oct 26, 1998
Owners & Moderators: David L. Gray and Richard Num
Other Moderators: Ezekiel MuAkil Bey, JReaves, Ralph L. McNeal,Jr.
Post message: pharesearch@yahoogroups.com
Subscribe: pharesearch-subscribe@yahoogroups.com
Unsubscribe: pharesearch-unsubscribe@yahoogroups.com
List owner: pharesearch-owner@yahoogroups.com

Philalethes - yahoogroup
Closed and Private Email List for Members of The Philalethes Society
Owner & Moderator: Nelson King
Related Link: http://groups.yahoo.com/group/philalethes
Post message: philalethes@yahoogroups.com
Subscribe: philalethes-subscribe@yahoogroups.com

Unsubscribe: philalethes-unsubscribe@yahoogroups.com
List owner: philalethes-owner@yahoogroups.com
Members (as of September 2005): 448
Founded: Dec 9, 1999

Philosophical Freemasonry - yahoogroup
We are a discussion forum, created for the purpose in keeping the traditional mysteries of Freemasonry as they were before. The main agenda here is esotericism, philosophy, and the ancient mysteries as they are intertwined with our sacred organization. There are the written as well as the oral traditions in Masonry, it is our duty to understand and preserve the oral, which is an endangered topic, with this we must also understand the written. In discussion will be the symbolic teachings, and the allegorical meanings of the craft. Only Master Masons of a regular Masonic Jurisdiction, interested in Philosophy, the seven liberal arts, and ancient mystery systems as they pertain to our order. This is strict Fraternal forum for members of the Organization only. Love and light. For in much wisdom [is] much grief: and he that increaseth knowledge increaseth sorrow. Eccle. 1:18
Members (as of September 2005): 150
Founded: May 1, 2004
Post message: Philosophical-Freemasonry@yahoogroups.com
Subscribe: Philosophical-Freemasonry-subscribe@yahoogroups.com
Unsubscribe: Philosophical-Freemasonry-unsubscribe@yahoogroups.com
List owner: Philosophical-Freemasonry-owner@yahoogroups.com

Pietre-Stones - yahoogroup
This "forum" is intended to provide an opportunity for Freemasons and persons interested in more information about history of Freemasonry and/or its influence in Architecture, Literature, Music and Art to get together and discuss their interests and share information. The list has been established only

for messages and short articles,papers regarding the topics stated: History of Freemasonry, Architecture and Freemasonry, Literature and Freemasonry, Music and Freemasonry, Art and Freemasonry, Masonic Symbolism and Rituals. Please, remember : it is not a list to exchange masonic information tout court. In Memoriam: This list is dedicated to W.Bro George Helmer passed to the GLA on February 18, 2002 at the age of 45 years. He was a Past Master of Norwood Lodge #90 A.F. ; A.M. G.R.A.Canada. Fellow of Philaletes Society. Moderator of the list since the foundation. His bright light reached far and wide.
W.Bro George Helmer, Moderator Emeritus
W.Bro Donald Falconer, Moderator
W.Bro Bruno V. Gazzo, List Owner
Related Link: http://www.freemasons-freemasonry.com/star.html
Post message: pietre-stones@yahoogroups.com
Subscribe: pietre-stones-subscribe@yahoogroups.com
Unsubscribe: pietre-stones-unsubscribe@yahoogroups.com
List owner: pietre-stones-owner@yahoogroups.com
Members (as of September 2005): 991
Founded: Sep 29, 1998

Prince Hall - yahoogroup
We are the oldest Prince Hall E-Mailing on the Internet. From Comm64 to Comp-U-Serv to AOL to Listbot and now here. The continuous design of this Prince Hall Masonry(E mail list) is to give people who enjoy Prince Hall Freemasonry a forum in which to quickly and easily get help, exchange ideas, and just sit back and socialize about Prince Hall Freemasonry.
Group Moderator: princehall-owner@egroups.com
To subscribe, send a message to princehall-subscribe@egroups.com or go to this e-group's home page at http://www.egroups.com/list/princehall
Members (as of September 2005): 961
Founded: Nov 11, 1998
Related Link: http://www.geocities.com/princehall_us/
Post message: princehall@yahoogroups.com

Subscribe: princehall-subscribe@yahoogroups.com
Unsubscribe: princehall-unsubscribe@yahoogroups.com
List owner: princehall-owner@yahoogroups.com
Owner & Moderator: Terrence CJ Williams
Other Moderator: Byron E. Hams

Royal Arch Masonry - yahoogroup
An email discussion list for the dissemination of educational
materials and free discussion of issues related to the Royal Arch.
Members (as of September 2005): 209
Founded: Nov 20, 2001
Post message: royalarch@yahoogroups.com
Subscribe: royalarch-subscribe@yahoogroups.com
Unsubscribe: royalarch-unsubscribe@yahoogroups.com
List owner: royalarch-owner@yahoogroups.com
Owner & Moderator: CJ Ferry

Shriners- 2000 - yahoogroup
(Shriners AAONMS) Originally beginning in 1999 as the unique
idea of just one Shrine Noble from Detroit, Shriners-2000 has
now blossomed into the premier Shrine listserver of our time,
currently serving over 900 Shrine Nobles from 158 Shrine
Temples. This is the one you've heard them "buzzing" about at
all the conventions! An exciting new interactive network exclu-
sively for Shriners. It's fun, it's interesting, it's easy to use, and
it's completely free of charge! Shriners-2000 is run by Shriners,
for Shriners. We're often imitated, but never duplicated. This is
the original private forum for Shriners only here in North
America and beyond, to express their thoughts and opinions,
and exchange ideas concerning the future of the Shrine as we
enter the 21st Century. Hopefully by working together, we can
make the Shrine Fraternity thrive and grow stronger through
knowledge and understanding. Here's what some members have
said about Shriners-2000 ... "We're Nobles helping Nobles in
the true spirit of the Shrine." ... "We're taking on the really tough
questions, and working together to find the answers." Shriners-
2000 is provided to Shriners free of charge. Membership is open

to all Shriners regardless of their Shrine Temple location. Shriners-2000 is for Shriners only! Credentials will be checked! (Shriners (A.A.O.N.M.S. only) of Masonic origin) Please allow 3 working days for membership approval.
Members (as of September 2005): 932
Founded: Jun 27, 1999
Related Link:
http://www.shrinershq.org/shrinersonly/sogeneral.html
Post message: Shriners-2000@yahoogroups.com
Subscribe: Shriners-2000-subscribe@yahoogroups.com
Unsubscribe: Shriners-2000-unsubscribe@yahoogroups.com
List owner: Shriners-2000-owner@yahoogroups.com
Owner & Moderator: Ed Rorick

UFVL - yahoogroup
This is a meeting place for all Freemasons, regardless of their Obedience. Your thoughts are invited. Mutual respect is a must. There are no gender restrictions. Freemasonry is a brotherhood working with traditional symbols & rituals. Its goals include:
* Helping its members to improve themselves
* Working for the brotherhood of all people with deep tolerance and respect for difference
* Promoting academic research into Freemasonry
* Supporting democracy, freedom, and human dignity
* Practicing assistance within the Craft, and service to the community.
As [br] Saint Exupéry once stated: Si tu diffères de moi, mon frère, loin de me lèser, tu m'enrichis.
Members (as of September 2005): 92
Founded: Dec 5, 2003
Post message: UFVL@yahoogroups.com
Subscribe: UFVL-subscribe@yahoogroups.com
Unsubscribe: UFVL-unsubscribe@yahoogroups.com
List owner: UFVL-owner@yahoogroups.com
Owner & Moderator: John Slifko

Women and Freemasonry - yahoogroup
This is a place for women freemasons and their supporters across the world to meet and exchange their masonic experiences, to learn more about each other and to keep in touch.
Members (as of September 2005): 39
Founded: Apr 7, 2001
Post message: womenandfm@yahoogroups.com
Subscribe: womenandfm-subscribe@yahoogroups.com
Unsubscribe: womenandfm-unsubscribe@yahoogroups.com
List owner: womenandfm-owner@yahoogroups.com
Owner & Moderator: Christine Chapman

"Yahoo Grand Lodge #1 F&AM" - yahoogroup
Yahoo Grand Lodge No. 1 F & AM is the first Internet Grand Lodge created on June 7th, 2002, in order to provide an interface between Freemasons from around the globe and from different Rites and Constitutions and have discussions about Freemasonry with them and with Non-Masons who are curious or have interest in the Craft. To achieve this members of Yahoo Grand Lodge have been running a chat room on yahoo called "Freemasonry Chat - On The Level" over the past five years and more. This chatroom was the inspiration behind the formation of Yahoo Grand Lodge. M.W.Bro. William R. Fischer officiated as the first Grand Master, followed by M.W.Bro. James Deans, who succeeded him on 30th June 2003, followed by MW Sis. Betty Langenberg who was elected to the office of Grand Master on 18th July, 2004. On 22nd June, 2005 our ruling Grand Master M.W. Bro Ambarish Singh Roy was elected and Installed to the office. Our Object is not to get more men into masonry, but to get more masonry into men.
Members (as of September 2005): 79
Founded: Jul 8, 2003
Post message: ygrandlodge@yahoogroups.com
Subscribe: ygrandlodge-subscribe@yahoogroups.com
Unsubscribe: ygrandlodge-unsubscribe@yahoogroups.com
List owner: ygrandlodge-owner@yahoogroups.com

Appendix D
Masonic Abbreviations

A&AR = Ancient & Accepted Rite (Scottish Rite)

AAONMS = Ancient Arabic Order Nobles of the Mystic Shrine (Shriners)

AASR = Ancient & Accepted Scottish Rite or Ancient Accepted Scottish Rite (without the &)

AEAONMS = Ancient Egyptian Arabic Order, Nobles Mystic Shrine (Prince Hall Shriners)

AEOS = Ancient Egyptian Order of Sciots

AF&AM = Ancient Free & Accepted Masons

AFHR = American Federation of Human Rights (Co-Masonry)

AFM = Ancient Free Masons (South Carolina)

AGL = Assistant Grand Lecturer

AGSW = Assistant Grand Superintendant of Workings (Australia)

ALR = American Lodge of Research (New York)

AMD = Allied Masonic Degrees

AQC = Ars Quatuor Coronatorum (transactions of English research lodge)

AYM = Ancient York Masons

Bro = Brother

CBCS = Chevaliers Biefaisants de La City Sainte (Holy Order of Knights Beneficient of the Holy City)

CH or COH = Captain of the Host (Royal Arch)

Comp = Companion (Royal Arch and Cryptic Rite, or Royal and Select Masters)

CWLR = Civil War Lodge of Research (chartered in Virginia)

DC = Director of Ceremonies

DGL = District Grand Lecturer

DDGL = District Deputy Grand Lecturer

DDGM = District Deputy Grand Master

DEO = District Education Officer

DGCHAP = Deputy Grand Chaplain

DGDC = Deputy Grand Director of Ceremonies

DGIW = Deputy Grand Inspector of Workings (Work)
DGM = Deputy Grand Master
DGZ = Deputy Grand Zerubbabel (First Grand Principal)
DH = Droit Humain (Co-Masonry)
DIW = District Instructor of Work
EA = Entered Apprentice
EC = Excellent Companion (Royal Arch) or Excellent Chief
    (Knight Masons) or English Constitution or Eminent
    Commander
EHP = Excellent High Priest (Royal Arch)
EO = Education Officer
F&AM = Free & Accepted Masons
FAAM = Free And Accepted Masons
FAAYM = Free and Accepted Ancient York Masons
FC = Fellowcraft or Fellow Craft
FPOF = Five Points of Fellowship
FPS = Fellow of the Philalethes Society or Fellow of the Phylaxis
    Society or Fellow of Phyllis Chapter
GAOTU = Great Architect of the Universe
GC = Grand Chief (Knight Masons)
GCR = Grand College of Rites
GHP = Grand High Priest (Royal Arch)
GJD = Grand Junior Deacon
GJS = Grand Junior Steward
GJW = Grand Junior Warden
GK = Grand King (Royal Arch)
GL = Grand Lodge or Grand Lecturer
GLF or GLoF or GLdF = Grand Lodge of France
GLFB = Feminine Grand Lodge of Belgium (Grande Loge
    Feminine de Belgique)
GLFF = Feminine Grand Lodge of France
GLNF = National Grand Lodge of France (Grand Loge Nationale
    Francais)
GM = Grand Master
GOF = Grand Orient of France
GS or GSec = Grand Secretary (or GS could be Grand Scribe)
GSD = Grand Senior Deacon

GSS = Grand Senior Steward

GSW = Grand Senior Warden or Grand Superintendant of
       Workings (Australia)

GWMNM or GWM = George Washington Masonic National
       Memorial (located in Alexandria, Virginia)

HA = Hiram Abif or Abiff

HP = High Priest (Royal Arch)

HRA = Holy Royal Arch

HRAKTP = Holy Royal Arch Knight Templar Priests

HTWSSTKS = abbreviation used in Royal Arch Masonry to
       describe someone in the Royal Arch ritual

IGH = Inspector General Honorary (33rd degree)

IM = Illustrious Master (Cryptic Rite, or Royal and Select
       Masters)

IOJD = International Order of Jobs Daughters

IORG = International Order of the Rainbow for Girls

IPR = Initiation, Passing, and Raising

JD = Junior Deacon

JGD = Junior Grand Deacon

JGS = Junior Grand Steward

JGW = Junior Grand Warden

JMC = Junior Master of Ceremonies

JS = Junior Steward

JW = Junior Warden

K = King (Royal Arch)

KCCH = Knight Commander of the Court of Honor (Scottish
       Rite)

KM = Knight Mason or Knight Masons

KT = Knights Templar

KTP = Knight Templar Priest

KYCH = Knight of the York Cross of Honor

LDH = Le Droit Humain (Co-Masonry)

LEO = Lodge Education Officer

LIW = Lodge Instructor of Work

M&M = Memphis & Misraim

MasEd = Masonic Education or Masonic Education Yahoo
       Group on the Internet

MBBFMN = Masonic Brotherhood of the Blue Forget Me Not (recognition of those involved in Masonic education)

MC = Master of Ceremonies or Middle Chamber

MCL = Middle Chamber Lecture

ME = Most Excellent (Royal Arch)

MEC = Most Excellent Companion (Royal Arch)

MEGHP = Most Excellent Grand High Priest (Royal Arch)

MEM = Most Excellent Master (Royal Arch)

MIC = Masonic Information Center (related to MSA - Masonic Service Association)

MIGM = Most Illustrious Grand Master (Cryptic Rite)

MLC = Masonic Leadership Center

MLMA = Masonic Library & Museum Association

MM = Master Mason or Mark Master

Mon = Monarch (Grotto)

MOS = Moment of Silence

MOVPER = Mystic Order of Veiled Prophets of the Enchanted Realm (Grotto)

MPS Member of the Philalethes Society or Member of the Phylaxis Society or Member of Phyllis Chapter

MSA = Masonic Service Association

MSANA = Masonic Service Association of North America

MSRICF = Masonic Societas Rosicruciana in Civitatibus Foederatis

MW = Most Worshipful

MWA = Masters and Wardens Association

MWB = Most Worshipful Brother

MWGL = Most Worshipful Grand Lodge

MWGM = Most Worshipful Grand Master

NCRL = Northern California Research Lodge

NECOMELI = Northeast Conference on Masonic Education & Libraries

NMJ = Northern Masonic Jurisdiction (Scottish Rite)

OES = Order of the Eastern Star

PAGSW = Past Assistant Grand Superintendant of Workings (Australia)

PDDGL = Past District Deputy Grand Lecturer

PDDGM = Past District Deputy Grand Master

PGBHQ = Past Grand Bethel Honored Queen (Job's Daughters)

PGHP = Past Grand High Priest (Royal Arch)

PGM = Past Grand Master

PGSW = Past Grand Superintendant of Workings (Australia)

PHA = Prince Hall Affiliated

PHO = Prince Hall Origin (National Compact) - NOT the same
    as PHA

PHQ = Past Honored Queen (Job's Daughters)

PIM = Past Illustrious Master (Cryptic Rite)

PM = Past Master

PMA = Past Masters Association

Pot = Potentate (Shrine)

POTS = Parting on the Square (sometimes used in place of
    "sincerely" in email messages from one Mason to another)

PS = Principal Sojourner (Royal Arch)

PSOC = Philalethes Society

PW = Password

RA = Royal Arch

RAC = Royal Arch Captain

RAM = Royal Arch Mason or Masonry or Royal Ark Mariner

RE = Right Excellent (Royal Arch) or Rite Emuulation
    (Emulation Rite)

REAA = Rite Ecossais Ancien et Accepte - (Ancient and Accepted
    Scottish Rite)

Rec = Recorder

REC = Right Excellent Companion (Royal Arch)

RER = Rite Ecossais Rectifie (Scottish Rectified Rite)

RF = Rite Français (French Rite)

ROS = Royal Order of Scotland

RW = Right Worshipful

RWB = Right Worshipful Brother

S = Scribe (Royal Arch)

S&C = Square and Compasses (or Compass)

S&F = Sincerely & Fraternally

SBF = Society of Blue Friars (association of Masonic authors)

SC = Scottish Constitution
SCRL = Southern California Research Lodge
SD = Senior Deacon
SEM = Super Excellent Master (Cryptic Rite)
SGC = Sovereign Grand Commander (Scottish Rite)
SGD = Senior Grand Deacon
SGIG = Sovereign Grand Inspector General (Scottish Rite)
SGS = Senior Grand Steward
SGW = Senior Grand Warden
SJ = Southern Jurisdiction (Scottish Rite)
SK = Sir Knight (Commandery and Knight Masons)
SMC = Senior Master of Ceremonies
SOF = soc.org.freemasonry (Masonic email group)
SRICF = Societas Rosicruciana in Civitatibus Foederatis (now
    called MSRICF - Masonic Societas Rosicruciana in
    Civitatibus Foederatis)
SRJ = Scottish Rite Journal
SRRS = Scottish Rite Research Society
SS = Senior Steward
STC = Supreme Tall Cedar
SW = Senior Warden
TCF = Tres Cher Frere (Very Dear Brother)
TIM = Thrice Illustrious Master (Royal and Select Masters)
QC = Quatuor Coronati Lodge No. 2076, London (research
    lodge - see AQC)
UD = Under Dispensation
UGLE = United Grand Lodge of England
UGLQ = United Grand Lodge of Queensland (Australia)
VSL = Volume of Sacred Law
VW = Very Worshipful
WB = Worshipful Brother
WM = Worshipful Master
WMA = Worshipful Masters Association
Wor = Worshipful

Appendix E
Masonic Book Publishers and Sellers
Publisher Information

Anchor Communications LLC
Ken Roberts
5266 Mary Ball Rd.
Lancaster, VA 22503
804-462-0384
email: kenroberts@goanchor.com
website: http://www.goanchor.com/

Berkelouw
830 N. Highland Ave
Los Angeles CA 90038
(phone) 213-466-3321

Charles T. Powner Company
Ezra A. Cook Publications Ltd.
6604 W. Irving Park Road
Chicago IL 60634
312-685-1101

Cornerstone Book Publishers
Michael Poll
Charlottesville, VA &
New Orleans, LA
email: info@cornerstonepublishers.com
website: http://www.cornerstonepublishers.com

Hiram Books
Duncan Publishing Group, LLC
P.O. Box 516
Denham Springs, LA 70726
Office: 225-791-3882 Fax: 225-612-6371
Email: info @ hirambooks.com
website: http://www.hirambooks.com

Ian Allan - Lewis Masonic
Riverdene Business Park
Molesey Road
Hersham, Surrey KT12 4RG
United Kingdom

M. Evans & Co., Inc.
216 East 49 St.
New York NY 10017

Macoy Publishing & Masonic Supply Co., Inc.
P.O. Box 9759
Richmond VA 23228-0759
phone: 804-262-6551   fax: 804-266-8256
email: custsvc@macoy.com
website: http://www.macoy.com

Global Masonic Publications
Kent Henderson
PO Box 36
Tailem Bend, SA 5260
Australia
tonypope@lm.net.au
website: http://www.geocities.com/kentgmp/

Kessinger Publishing, Inc.
P.O. Box 1404
Whitefish, MT 59937
website: http://www.kessingerpub.com/

Masonic Book Club
Robin L.Carr
1811 Hoover Drive
Normal, IL 61761-2202
rlcarr1@msn.com or rlcarr@ilstu.edu

Masonic Service Association
8120 Fenton St.
Silver Spring MD 20910

Philalethes Society
http://freemasonry.org/psoc/

Phylaxis Society
COFP Book Dept
c/o Robert N Campbell, FPS
10614 Bellefontaine
Kansas City, MO 64137-1737

Quatuor Coronati Correspondence Circle Ltd
60 Great Queen Street,
London WC2B 5BA
UK

Scottish Rite, Northern Masonic Jurisdiction
Supreme Council, NMJ
P.O. Box 519
Lexington, MA 02173

Scottish Rite, Southern Jurisdiction
1733 - 16th Street NW
Washington DC 20009
http://www.srmason-sj.org/web/index.htm

Southern California Research Lodge
Ralph Herbold
scrlfam@aol.com
PO Box 939
Ashland OR 97520
http://www.calodges.org/scrl

Templar Books
PO Box 5063
Hinton, Alberta
T7V 1X3
Canada
http://www.templarbooks.com

The Temple Books and Publishers
Joe Ohlandt
PO Box 1396
Morristown, New Jersey 07962-1396
973-898-3770
http://thetemplebooks.com/

Appendix E
U.S. National Masonic Appendant Bodies

Short Name / Official Name / Website

Amaranth
Supreme Council Order of the Amaranth Inc.
http://www.amaranth.org

AMD
The Grand Council Allied Masonic Degrees of the United States of America
http://www.alliedmasonicdegrees.org/

Bath
Order of the Bath of the United States of America

Blue Friars
The Society of Blue Friars
http://bessel.org/sbf.htm

CBCS
Chevaliers Biefaisants de La City Sainte (Holy Order of Knights Beneficient of the Holy City)

Corks
Ye Antient Order of Corks

Cryptic Masons
General Grand Council Cryptic Masons
http://www.yorkrite.com/council/cmdegrees.html

Daughters of Mokanna

Daughters of the Nile
http://www.daughtersofthenile.com/

DeMolay
Order of DeMolay
http://www.demolay.org/

Eastern Star
The General Grand Chapter, Order of the Eastern Star
http://www.easternstar.org/

Fire Fighters Square Club International
Fire Fighters Masonic Square Club

Golden Chain Order of the Golden Chain
http://njfreemasonry.org/chain.htm

Golden Key
Order of the Golden Key

Grand College of Rites
The Grand College of Rites of the U.S.A.
http://www.grandcollegeofrites.org/

Grotto
Mystic Order of Veiled Prophets of the Enchanted Realm
http://www.scgrotto.com

Heroes of '76 part of National Sojourners, Inc.

High Twelve International
http://www.gwu.edu/~fellows/high12.html

HRAKTP
Grand College of America,
Holy Royal Arch Knight Templar Priests
http://www.yorkrite.com/hraktp/

International Law Enforcement Officers' Square Club
http://www.angelfire.com/ny/lazaruslong/

Jesters
The Royal Order of Jesters

Job's Daughters
International Order of Job's Daughters
http://www.iojd.org/

Knights Templar
Grand Encampment of Knights Templar of the United States of America
http://www.knightstemplar.org/

Grand Encampment Knights Templar,
United States of America and Its Jurisdiction, Prince Hall Affiliation, Inc.

Knight Masons
Grand Council, Knight Masons U.S.A.
http://www.yorkrite.com/knightmasons/

KYCH
Knights of the York Cross of Honour
http://www.yorkrite.com/kych/

Ladies Oriental Shrine
Ladies Oriental Shrine of North America
http://www.unitylodge.com/appendantbodies/appendant_losna.html

Masonic Book Club
rlcarr1@msn.com

Masonic Poets Society
http://home.midmaine.com/~gleighton/

National Camping Travelers, Inc.
http://www.gonct.org/

National League of Masonic Clubs
http://hometown.aol.com/JSchofi863/

National Sojourners
National Sojourners, Inc.
http://www.nationalsojourners.org/

Philalethes Society
http://freemasonry.org/psoc/

Phylaxis Society
http://freemasonry.org/phylaxis/

Phyllis Chapter
The Phyllis Chapter of the Phylaxis Society
http://freemasonry.org/phyllis/

Poetry International
Masonic Poetry Society
http://www.masonic-poetry.org/

Masonic Poets Society

Quetzalcoatl
Order of Quetzalcoatl

Rainbow Girls
International Order of the Rainbow for Girls
http://www.iorg.org/

Red Cross of Constantine
http://www.yorkrite.com/rcc/

Rosicrucians (MSRICF)
Masonic Societas Rosicruciana in Civitatibus Foederatis
http://www.yorkrite.com/msricf/
http://www.geocities.com/Athens/2092/ (California College)

Royal Arch
General Grand Chapter Royal Arch Masons International
http://yorkrite.com/chapter/

General Conference Grand Chapters,
Holy Royal Arch Masons, Prince Hall Affiliation,
United States and The Bahamas

Royal Order of Scotland
The Royal Order of Scotland,
The Provincial Grand Lodge United States of America
http://www.yorkrite.com/roos/info.html

Sciots
Ancient Egyptian Order of Sciots
http://www.sciots.org/

Scottish Rite, Northern Masonic Jurisdiction
The Ancient Accepted Scottish Rite for the Northern Masonic
Jurisdiction of the United States of America
http://www.supremecouncil.org/

Scottish Rite, Southern Jurisdiction
Supreme Council, 33°, Scottish Rite of Freemasonry, Southern
Jurisdiction, USA
http://www.srmason-sj.org/web/index.htm

Shrine
Ancient Arabic Order of the Nobles of the Mystic Shrine
http://shrinershq.org

Social Order of Beauceants

Tall Cedars
Tall Cedars of Lebanon of North America
http://www.tallcedars.org/

True Kindred
Order of the True Kindred
http://www.shawneemasoniclodge54.com/True%20Kindred/

White Shrine of Jerusalem
The Order of the White Shrine of Jerusalem
http://www.calodges.org/no194/WSJ93/Flyer/Flyer.htm

York Rite College
York Rite Sovereign College of North America
http://www.yorkrite.com/yrscna/

About the Author

Paul M. Bessel, 33°, is currently (2005) Senior Grand Warden of the Grand Lodge of Washington DC (District of Columbia), and a Past Master, Member, and Honorary member of Lodges in Washington DC, Virginia, and New York, and of most of the Masonic appendant and concordant bodies. He was one of the founders and a Past Master of the Civil War Lodge of Research #1865, District Deputy Grand Master for Research Lodges in Virginia, and Past President of the Masonic Library and Museum Association. He is a Fellow and Life Member of the Scottish Rite Research Society and the Philalethes Society and Executive Secretary of the Allen E. Roberts Masonic Leadership Center.

Paul is well known in "computer Masonry." He is the founder and moderator of Masonic email message groups and maintains extensive websites for Masonic education. He is also the author of many articles in Masonic publications and a speaker on varied topics at many Masonic meetings.

Paul was born in 1949 in Brooklyn, New York. He is currently a resident of Silver Spring, Maryland, where he is a lawyer for Youth Leaders International (YLI), a foundation that brings together high school students from many countries for education, leadership training, and appreciation of the universality of all people.

Printed in the United States
93256LV00007B/152/A

9 781887 560597